GR 271 .K85 E34 2008
Edgecomb, Diane.
A fire in my heart

MHCC WITHDRAWN

D1737409

A Fire in My Heart

World Folklore Advisory Board

Simon J. Bronner, Ph.D.
Distinguished Professor of Folklore and American Studies
Pennsylvania State University at Harrisburg

Joseph Bruchac, Ph.D.
Abenaki Storyteller and Writer

Natalie O. Kononenko, Ph.D.
Professor of Slavic Language and Literature
University of Virginia

Norma J. Livo, Ed.D.
Writer and Storyteller

Margaret Read MacDonald, Ph.D.
King County Library System

A Fire in My Heart

Kurdish Tales

Retold by Diane Edgecomb

With Contributions by Mohammed M. A. Ahmed and Çeto Ozel
and Original Illustrations by Rebekah Murphy

World Folklore Series

LIBRARIES UNLIMITED
UNLIMITED
A Member of the Greenwood Publishing Group

Westport, Connecticut • London

Library of Congress Cataloging-in-Publication Data

Edgecomb, Diane.
  A fire in my heart : Kurdish tales / retold by Diane Edgecomb ; with contributions
  by Mohammed M. A. Ahmed and Çeto Ozel.
    p. cm. — (World folklore series)
  Includes bibliographical references and index.
  ISBN-13: 978-1-59158-437-7 (alk. paper)
  1. Tales—Kurdistan. 2. Tales—Turkey, Eastern. 3. Kurds—Folklore. I.
Ahmed, Mohammed M. A. II. Ozel, Çeto. III. Title.
GR271.K85E34   2008
398.2095667—dc22   2007028810

British Library Cataloguing in Publication Data is available.

Copyright © 2008 by Diane Edgecomb

All rights reserved. No portion of this book may be
reproduced, by any process or technique, without the
express written consent of the publisher. Exceptions
include reproduction and performance in educational,
not-for-profit settings.

Library of Congress Catalog Card Number: 2007028810
ISBN-13: 978-1-59158-437-7

First published in 2008

Libraries Unlimited, 88 Post Road West, Westport, CT 06881
A Member of the Greenwood Publishing Group, Inc.
www.lu.com

Printed in the United States of America

The paper used in this book complies with the
Permanent Paper Standard issued by the National
Information Standards Organization (Z39.48–1984).

10 9 8 7 6 5 4 3 2 1

The publisher has done its best to make sure the instructions and/or recipes in this book are correct.
However, users should apply judgment and experience when preparing recipes, especially parents
and teachers working with young people. The publisher accepts no responsibility for the outcome of
any recipe included in this volume.

This book is dedicated to the brave and soulful people of Kurdistan.
Her bijîn.

Contents

Foreword

The Kurdish culture is ancient and rich, containing myriad songs, traditions, dances, and stories that preserve echoes of Kurdistan's recent and distant past. Although Kurdish literature dates back to pre-Islamic times, written pieces such as the classic love story *Mem û Zin* by Ehmedê Xanî written in 1695, *Mewluda Kurdî* and the epic poem *Zembîlfrosh* by Mele Ehmedê Bateyî (1417–1491) and the works of Kurdish poets such as Baba Tahir (1000–1054), Eliyê Herirî (1425–1490), and Feqiyeê Teyran (1590–1660) are precious rarities. In some cases, only fragments of older written materials remain. Kurdistan was often at the center of wars between surrounding powers. Invading armies often destroyed libraries and the buildings that housed them. In recent times, the oppressive policies of hostile governments have forced most Kurds to be more concerned with the preservation of life than with the preservation of their ancient culture. Kurds have been surviving execution of their intellectuals, burning of their villages, forced assimilation policies, bombardment with poison gas, disappearances, deportations and a seemingly unending parade of wars and conflicts.

Most of the stories in this book were collected in the Kurdish region of Turkey, a region where intellectual oppression can be daily and extreme and where, starting from the foundation of the Turkish Republic in 1923, the Kurdish language has been officially banned by law 2932 in the Turkish Penal Code (this law was removed in 1992). Because of this, what has been preserved of the culture is found mainly in the older generation. There, sung by our singers (dengbêj) and recounted by our tellers of tales (çîrokbêj) you will find the centuries-old legends, folk tales and epic story-songs of the Kurds. History lives in these sung epics. Often the story-songs of the dengbêj immortalized historic events. Tales of bravery became legends through dramatization in verse.

I remember well the context in which these tales were traditionally told in simple villages high up in the mountains. Until recently, these villages had no modern conveniences, no electricity, and no television. Because of this, one of the greatest joys was gathering together for the sharing of stories. Stories were told during the long nights of winter, as there was time for little else besides work in the other three seasons. Most Kurds can tell you reminiscences of these times. For the millions of Kurds of the diaspora, these remembrances hold a deep and special place in the heart.

Imagine, if you will, how it was when the ground was deeply covered in snow. Despite all the natural hardships, winter was the most beautiful and relaxing season of the year, as the roads were closed and the villagers were able to enjoy their freedom without outside interference for six to seven months.

After a long day tending livestock in snowy fields and in barns away from the village location, the villagers would come home one by one. They would take off their wet woolen socks, and shelwars (baggy trousers); wash their face, hands, and feet; and wait for the other members of the family to come together for stews such as tirshik, keledosh, or dohîn (a yogurt soup). The ingredients for these dishes consisted of dried mountain plants gathered in the summer, as well as various grains, nuts, yogurt, and sometimes meat. When there was a guest, tirshik, a favorite dish, would be served. Tirshik consists of kifte (bulgar dumplings filled with ground walnuts or meat) cooked in a rich stew of onions, sumac, chickpeas, tomato paste, and karî, a flavorful vegetable of the mountain. We would always know when a guest had arrived because the house would be filled with the wonderful scent of the karî.

In the evening, the whole family would come together and sit to eat around a piece of cloth covering the handwoven carpets on the floor. Not only the immediate family but also the extended family would gather, for they often lived nearby or even under the same roof. A large flat piece of lavshe (flatbread) made from homegrown wheat and baked in the tandoor (a clay-lined pit oven) would be given to everyone, and the dinner would begin.

After dinner there would be the drinking of tea and then a search to find some entertainment for the long winter's night. Some would play gustîlanê, a team game in which a ring or other object is hidden under walnut shells. Then, amid a lot of laughter, one of the teams tries to discover under which shell the ring is hiding. Some would play chess, or dama (draughts), while others might wrap up and go on foot to another village, even in a snowstorm, to listen to the tales told by different storytellers. No one was expected to have an invitation to visit anyone else's house. In these small villages everyone was familiar, and guests were always welcome. In fact, the arrival of a newcomer was a welcome delight. The mêvan (guest) would be expected to stay at least a day at many different houses.

Sometimes when an important visiting storyteller came from another region, the whole village would come together for this special occasion. The biggest house was often chosen as the place to hear the new stories the guest might have. Stories were usually told in a room especially designed for receiving company. A bright lamp called a lux, reserved for visiting tellers, would be brought out, and everyone would sit in a circle around the room on soft cushions that were wrapped in colorful handwoven woolen carpets. Large pillows supported the back. For warmth, there was a wood stove in the middle of the room. The storyteller would sit in a central place so that the whole audience could see him tell the story, sing songs based on it, and sometimes even act out dramatic parts. The audience would ask the storyteller to tell them their favorite story or a new story they had never heard before.

Storytelling would start at seven in the evening and continue until eleven or twelve at night. If the story hadn't finished, the audience and the storyteller would meet the subsequent day or days, so there was always the next part of the story to look forward to. As the days passed, they would continue to enjoy the unfolding of these epics.

The stories usually centered on themes of love or heroism. There were also true tales and a recounting of the events that happened in important wars. While the story was being told, the audience was usually silent. Sometimes, however, they would show their emotions by pitying, praising or cursing the characters. Some would cry silently at a tragic ending. You would know only by seeing the tears falling down their cheeks. At various times, the elders would ask the storyteller questions to help sum up the story and clarify the relationship between characters so that everyone could take in all the details. Since the stories told were quite long, there were intervals where tea and snacks such as winter pears that had been preserved in oak leaves, walnuts, raisins, honey, or keshk (dried yogurt) were served.

There were stories for everyone and for every occasion. For example, if someone was dishonest while trading with others, the story of the origin of the turtle would come up. "The turtle was actually a man who owned a mill. He gave his customers less flour than they deserved by using a smaller bowl as a measurement tool. So Xwedê (kweh-day) punished him by putting that bowl upside down on his back and turning him into a turtle forever." Elderly women within the family usually told short animal stories. Almost every mother or grandmother could tell the children short stories and the children would fall asleep in the lap of an aunt or elderly relative, their hair being gently stroked as the story wove on and on.

Never can I forget those long white nights. Everywhere, the fields, the mountains, the trees were full of snow like a white sheet that brightened the darkest nights.

This storytelling tradition along with our celebratory and seasonal songs and dances is deeply threatened. Nowadays, Kurds are suffering the loss of the villages that once preserved their language and culture. According to official figures released by the Turkish National Assembly Human Rights Commission four to five thousand villages have been burned down and the inhabitants of these villages displaced in the last twenty years. These figures do not reflect the additional four thousand villages which, according to Minority Rights Group International, were destroyed by Saddam Hussein's Ba'athist regime. As a result of these atrocities, five million Kurds living in Kurdistan have been displaced both internally and externally and dispersed all over the world.

Only in the southern part of Kurdistan (Iraq), since the formation of the Kurdistan Regional Government in 1992, have Kurdish language and identity flourished. There, Kurdish children have been educated in their mother tongue in all educational institutions starting from kindergarten to university education. However, in other regions of Kurdistan, language oppression is severe. Although Kurds living in the northwest of Kurdistan (Turkey) have a population of about fifteen to twenty million, they don't have the right to education in their native language. Kurds living in the eastern part of Kurdistan (Iran) also have no right to education in Kurdish. The recent changes that have been made to these policies have only been cosmetic and formalistic. In the southwestern part of Kurdistan, controlled by Syria, Kurds have no rights at all. Many are not even accepted as citizens of that country. They have never been given ID cards and are looked upon as refugees, even though they are living on their native land.

If children of a nation do not acquire a proper knowledge of their mother tongue during an educational process starting from primary school to university education, they cannot maintain their identity. The demise of an ancient Indo-European language and culture is approaching fast unless Kurds, a nation with a population of forty million, are given their right to self-determination like other people enjoying this right in the world.

The stories, poetry, songs, ritual speech, literature, and syntax of a language store the collective intellectual achievements of a culture and supply us with unique perspectives on fundamental problems of the human condition. When a language disappears, all of these insights and perspectives, along with the major medium that sustains and reinvigorates a culture, are lost. I hope this book full of wonderful Kurdish stories will remind readers that this unique treasure belongs to all mankind and that its disappearance will constitute an irretrievable loss to us all.

—Çeto Ozel

December 2006

Rastî bibe derzî jî naşkê

Truth can be needle-like, hidden yet impossible to shatter.

—Kurdish Proverb

Preface

The Kurds, one of the indigenous peoples of the Middle East, are also one of the least known. Part of this is because the remote mountainous landscape they have inhabited with strength and tenacity for centuries has kept them isolated from the world. Theirs is a voice that has all too often been silenced or ignored. At present, the Kurds are the largest ethnic group in the world without their own nation-state; still they consider themselves a nation and call their homeland Kurdistan.

The area known as Kurdistan is transnational and contiguous, straddling Iraq, Iran, Syria, and Turkey. Although there are occasions in this book where Kurdistan is referred to in general terms simply as "Kurdistan," the more specific designations Iraqi Kurdistan, Syrian Kurdistan, Iranian Kurdistan, and Turkish Kurdistan are also used. In a few rare cases, the compass directions of north, south, east, and west will appear before the word *Kurdistan* as an aid to visualization. The map will help to clarify the location of the various places referred to.

In keeping with the desire to create a book for the general public from the Kurdish perspective, when describing locations, Kurdish names and older place-names usually precede current regional names. Where strict usage of the Latin Kurdish alphabet would have impeded a search for more information about a particular place, I have resorted to current anglicizations of these older place-names. This usually involved substituting the Kurdish "c" with the more phonetic "j" sound. For example "Halbca" has been included on the map as "Halabja." Kurdish is a language that is still being standardized; because of this there may be discrepancies in spelling from one source to another.

The outlines of the map of Kurdistan were taken from two sources: first, a map produced by the CIA in 1992 depicting areas with a Kurdish majority and, second, the map of Kurdistan presented by the Kurdish league Xoybun (Khoybun) to the first session of the United Nations at the end of World War II. Xoybun, a political entity created in 1919 by a group of Kurdish intellectuals, declared the first Kurdish government in exile in 1927. Of course one map cannot take into account the displacement of large groups of people such as the forced exodus of the Armenians from Van and other regions of Turkey that occurred in 1915–1918. It also does not take into account recent displacements of the Kurds, for example, forced relocations under the "Arabization" policies of Saddam Hussein's regime in Iraq. For additional maps and a greater appreciation of the homeland of the Kurds, I refer

the reader to Maria T. O'Shea's *Trapped between the Map and Reality* and Mehrdad R. Izady's *The Kurds: A Concise Handbook.*

I collected the stories in this book between 1999 and 2006 in large part from the Kurdish region of Turkey. When others have collected or contributed stories, this information has been included in the notes section at the end of that particular tale. As often as possible, I have noted year of collection and region of the teller along with age, gender and Kurdish dialect.

There are several Kurdish dialects: Kurmancî (Kurmanjî), Soranî, Dimilî (or Zazakî), and Goranî. When the Kurdish language is used or referred to in this book, it is almost exclusively the Kurmancî dialect, the dialect that is spoken by a majority of the Kurdish people. In some cases, where Kurdish words appear by themselves, I have substituted anglicized phonetic letterings so that the reader can more easily sound out the word. Common phonetic substitutions are "kh" for the Kurdish letter "x" and "sh" for the Kurdish letter "ş." When the Kurdish language is used in specific phrases, as it is in the proverbs, these words are spelled out using the current Latin alphabet for Kurmancî. As an aid to those who would like to pronounce the Kurdish words, I have included a basic phonetics chart as an appendix. For a more in-depth exploration of the unique sounds of the Kurdish language, I suggest either Baran Rizgar's *Kurdish-English Dictionary* or Michael Chyet's recently published *Kurdish-English Dictionary.*

I have been lucky enough to work with a variety of Kurdish translators, all of them native speakers. They imparted a great deal of cultural information that provided context for the tales. When working with the stories, I began with my transcriptions of their oral translations. The tales were then retold with an eye to clarity and flow in the English language. In some happy cases, I was able to work from several variations of the same tale. When a translator is not credited, it is because the individual has requested that his or her name be withheld. The only stories with which I have not worked from oral translations are the following: "Sultan Mahmud and Heyas," contributed by Leeya Thompson, and "The Goranî Story of Rawchî," contributed by Mustafa Dehqan. "The Zay Tree and the Tay Falcon" is reprinted verbatim from the International Journal of Kurdish Studies.

As can often be the case with traditional material, some of the tales have violent episodes or present difficult themes. Because of this, educators and parents are encouraged to review the story material first to decide what is appropriate, especially when reading to younger children.

One last note, my focus in this book has been on the life of the "gund," the Kurdish village. In my experience, the gund is the heart of Kurdistan, the place where the stories, folklore, and traditions resonate and are preserved. In recent times, thousands of Kurdish villages have been deliberately destroyed by hostile governments. It remains to be seen whether the traditions of village life survive or are transformed. In the meantime, the Kurds turn their eyes to the south where, in the newly renovated cities of Iraqi Kurdistan, a new day is dawning.

So with an eye toward the past, present, and future, let's begin with the traditional introduction to a Kurdish story: Yek hebû û yek tûnebû . . . "Once there was and once there wasn't . . ."

—Diane Edgecomb

June 2007

Acknowledgments

I am faced with a beautiful dilemma: a wealth of gratitude. This project has been blessed from the start with lucky meetings, friendships, and unforeseen opportunities all along the way. Almost, you can say, it was meant to be. I will thank some in particular but also hold in my heart those I cannot name here—storytellers, translators, and others. There are many who are still in harm's way if they reveal that they pursue anything related to their Kurdish heritage. One day I hope to be able to state all of their names with the joy I feel as I think of their help.

I don't know whether to speak of Çeto Ozel first, last, or all through the acknowledgments. He has been with me from the moment I asked him to send me *Kurdiya Nûjen,* his book of Kurdish for beginners, many years ago. When I told him of this project, he joined me on the way, helping me every step with the creation of this book. His passion for and his knowledge of his culture and the Kurdish language deepened everything I attempted to do. His sense of humor always lightened the way. He has been my comrade, advisor, consultant, translator, contributor, and treasure trove of information. Zor spas, heval!

I wish to express my gratitude to Bêrîvan, Nuri, Himet, Cazya, and their entire family. Bêrîvan guided me via phone, all the way from London, finding those who could help me and sending me on to her little Kurdish village. Nuri was a true knight, helping me to collect and taking precious time to treat both my translator and myself as though we were visiting dignitaries. Bêrîvan's mother, Cazya, a supreme cook, delighted me with traditional meals and tales of how they prepared food in her village—in ways unchanged for hundreds of years. Thanks also to Abbas Alkan who gave me both his published and unpublished manuscripts of Kurdish stories to draw from—tales he bravely collected despite threats of violence. I am grateful as well to Nursen, Sajo, and their relatives who opened their homes to me in Mukus, a breathtakingly beautiful and remote Kurdish region, and to all of my dear friends in the New England Kurdish community, they welcomed me and encouraged me all along the way. Mehmet Bozbay from Gallery Mezopotamya in Van, Turkey, was a great support. He provided me with Kurdish tribal rugs to use as models for the abstract borders and motifs in this book and gave me invaluable help, counsel, and assistance all along the way.

One Kurdish man in particular I wish to thank. He must remain nameless but I affectionately call him "Indie" (after the adventurous character Indiana Jones). He guided me through the heart of Kurdistan, located most of my tellers, found ways to bring me to remote villages, and translated for hours on end. He put his heart, soul, and safety on the line for this project.

Stateside, I was helped by my brother, Robert Edgecomb, who, despite his difficult schedule, took time to coddle every photo in the book. No matter what the photo's age or resolution, he found a way to squeeze out as much detail and nuance as Photoshop and man will allow. My intrepid assistant, Rebekah Murphy, continued to rise to every challenge and created lovely versions of each illustration and graphic I asked for, including the difficult assignment of the map. For recipes, advice, and help I wish to thank Gulcem Aktas, Bêrîvan, Cazya, Nurcan Sarac, Dilshad Ozel, Maia and Andrew Mazlum Aytac, and Hanim Aytac. Thanks also to Sardar Jajan, Annet Henneman, Nachum Cohen—who never forgot his Kurdish roots—and Katherine Cipolla—who reviewed the recipe section and brought her extensive culinary expertise to my improvised "Kurdish test kitchen." For the contribution of games I thank Nurcan Sarac and Çeto Ozel. Lokman I. Meho, gracious and helpful as always, gave me suggestions for bibliographic resources.

Mehmet Akbas and Lokman Ablakhi coached me on the delicate and fraught matter of the map. They helped me to understand that a name is not just a name, and a place "welatê min" (my homeland) is a very deep thread in the psyche.

Thanks also to those who proofed and analyzed with such insight and precision, especially Maia Mesnil-Aytac, Tom Megan, Margot Chamberlain—who went over every inch of the manuscript—and my sister, Martha Malone, who put her fingers to the keyboard day after day during "crunch time" as I prepared the manuscript for submission.

My husband, Tom Megan, was wonderful as always, accompanying me when he could and supporting me every step of the way when he couldn't. My dreams were right when they told me he would be the one to help my visions become reality.

To the foundations that were willing to support something as risky as an "individual artist," I wish to give special thanks. Funds from the Ella Lyman Cabot Fund, the Sparkplug Foundation, and the National Storytelling Network helped make my dream of collecting a reality.

And there are those that started me on this journey, those who first opened my eyes and my heart to the Kurdish struggle, especially Adil Yalcin. The heartrending story of his journey as a refugee and his love for his homeland, Kurdistan, touched me so deeply that I was moved to action. And I cannot forget Hanim Aytac who, like most Kurds, carries the memory and the deep love of the Kurdish village with her. It was a life she was forced to leave, but for her it remained close and profound. "I never forget. It's like fire," she would often say as she held her fist close to her heart. Those memories burned for her, and as they burned she, with her fierce love, kept something precious alive. It is her words that have become the title of this book. Like many Kurds, in spite of the hardship they may have been through, they carry that fire always in their hearts.

—Diane Edgecomb

Some of the stories in this book are included by special arrangement with the holders of copyright and publication rights. I wish to thank those listed below for permissions granted:

Mustafa Dehqan who granted first publication rights and permission to retell the Goranî legend of "Rawchî"

Leeya Thompson who granted first publication rights and permission to retell the Soranî story "Sultan Mahmud, and Heyas"

The International Journal of Kurdish Studies for permission to reprint the Soranî legend "The Zay Tree and the Tay Falcon" from Volume 13, Number 2, "Kurdish Folktales" © 1999

Abbas Alkan who granted permission to translate into English, retell, and publish three stories from his Kurmancî Kurdish story collection *Çîroka Rovî û Gur* [*Tales of Fox and Wolf*]: "Rovî û Legleg" ("Fox and Stork"), "Rovî Bû Zembîl Firoş" ("Fox, the Basketmaker"), and "Pezê Ji Kêrî Biqete Nesîbê Gura Ye" ("The Sheep That Strays from the Flock Becomes the Wolf's Dinner")

For first publication rights of their photos I wish to thank:

Rudman Ham, who contributed photographs taken in Iraqi Kurdistan between 1954 and 1956,

Çeto Ozel, who contributed various photos, and

Tom Megan, who contributed the author photo and two scenic photos.

Pişta xwe bide an mêrekî çê an çiyakî asê.

Have at your back a brave man or a steep mountain.

—Kurdish Proverb

Introduction: A Brief History of the Kurdish People

Dr. Mohammed M. A. Ahmed

Two men in traditional dress, Iraqi Kurdistan, circa 1955. Photo courtesy of Rudman Ham.

History

The Kurds take pride in their history and cultural identity as a distinct group of people who have lived in the mountains, hills, and fertile valleys of Kurdistan for millennia. They have weathered Greek, Roman, Arab, Persian, and nomadic Turkish invaders from central Asia. Some historians have traced the history of these ancient people to some four thousand years ago, while some states that now occupy Kurdish lands tell us that these people do not exist and have never existed in the past. However, despite regional states' denial, Kurds and Kurdistan exist in the consciousness of all Kurds and their politicians and activists. Some historians believe that the Kardouchoi, mentioned in Xenophon's *Anabasis,* who mauled Alexander the Great's ten thousand soldiers as they retreated from Persia in 401 B.C.E. were the ancestors of the Kurds. The Kurds consider themselves descendents of the Medes who

overthrew the Assyrian Empire in 612 B.C.E. after the Assyrians ruled their land for some five hundred years (Herodotus 1942, 54–55). It was in the seventh century that the Arab Islamic invaders of Kurdistan applied the name *Kurd* to the people of the upper Mesopotamia.

Saladin

One of the most famous of all Kurds is the legendary King Saladin (1138–1193) respected by both Muslims and Christians for his fair treatment of his enemies (McDowall 1996, *A Modern History of the Kurds*, 3). Saladin's brilliant military campaign recaptured the lands taken by the Crusaders and led to the defeat of King Richard the Lion-Hearted. King Saladin has been immortalized in verse and legend as a model of chivalry because of the gallantry and magnanimity he displayed to the defeated Christian crusaders when he captured Jerusalem (Beaudin Saeedpour 1999, 56–59).

Historiography

Education was not easy to come by in the mountainous regions of Kurdistan, far from centers of excellence such as Constantinople, Damascus, and Baghdad. Perhaps because of this, a great deal of Kurdish history has been written by others, some of whom have much to gain by denying the Kurds their separate ethnic identity and their contribution to history. In the absence of adequate research by Kurds and Kurdologists, there is often a dearth of accurate information. Even the famous Saladin has been inaccurately referred to as being of Turkish or Arabic origin (Beaudin Saeedpour 1999, 56–59). In modern times, the denial of the existence of the Kurds has taken place on a state level. Turkey, considered a modern democracy by many, has for years pursued a policy of forced assimilation, denying the very existence of the Kurds, calling them "Mountain Turks," even falsely claiming that the Kurds' ancient Indo-European language is a dialect of Turkish. When pursuing the history of the Kurds, you must be persistent and look carefully and critically at the source.

Geography, Climate, and Resources

The Kurds call their homeland Kurdistan. It consists of rugged but beautiful snow-capped mountains and green valleys endowed with numerous lakes and streams that feed into the Tigris and Euphrates Rivers. It has a moderate climate: dry in summer and cold during the winter. Kurdistan is one of the richest parts of the Middle East in natural resources, especially oil, gas, farmland, and water. Kurdistan's rich farmlands produce an abundance of food for the neighboring communities, as far away as Ankara, Istanbul, Aleppo, Damascus, Baghdad, and Tehran.

Environment and Festival

One must see Kurdistan in March and early April to enjoy the sight of its colorful wild-flowers and meandering streams. It is then that one of the most important celebrations, the Kurdish New Year, takes place on March 21. This traditional gathering called Newroz (new day) is a time when everyone comes together to dance around great bonfires in colorful clothing. Young people often test their skill by leaping and turning elaborately over the flames, celebrating the day when, according to folk legend, their hero, the blacksmith Kawa, triumphed over the tyrant king, Dahak.

Language

Despite diverse Kurdish dialects, depending on which side of the rugged mountains or borders they live, most can easily communicate with each other. Kurdish, the language of the Kurds, is Indo-European and belongs to the Iranic branch spoken by Persians, Indians, Baluchs, and others living in south and southwest Asia. It is totally distinct from Arabic and Turkish.

History and Trade

While the Kurds consider themselves a nation—a distinct people with a common language, culture, and history—they have never had a unified nation-state of their own. However numerous Kurdish emirates (city-states), maintaining a great deal of independence, dotted their land even after the Ottoman and Persian Empires divided Kurdistan between them in the seventeenth century (Brisley 1994, 31–32). These early Kurdish city-states featured prominently in the region's economy. They were relied on to keep the thriving trade route, the "silk road" safe for the endless caravan of goods flowing between Europe and Asia.

Division of Kurdistan

Kurdistan was divided once in 1639 between the Ottoman and the Persian Safavid Empires and again after World War I when the Ottoman Empire fragmented. The breakup of the Ottoman Empire saw the greatest hope for the establishment of the Kurds' own nation-state. U.S. President Woodrow Wilson's Fourteen Point Programme for World Peace called for self-determination for the non-Turkish minorities formerly ruled by the Ottomans, specifically calling for the establishment of a Kurdish state. The Treaty of Sevre, written in 1920 to decide the future of the old Ottoman Empire, reflected Wilson's concerns by offering the establishment of an independent Kurdistan. Article 62 states: *"A Commission sitting at Constantinople . . . shall draft within six months from the coming into force of the present Treaty a scheme of local autonomy for the predominantly Kurdish areas lying east of the Euphrates, south of the southern boundaries of Armenia . . . and north of the frontier of Tur-*

key with Syria and Mesopotamia." Article 64 provided for the Kurdish region that was part of the former Ottoman vilayet of Mosul to join with the aforementioned independent Kurdish state.

Unfortunately for the Kurds, the new Turkish republic, led by Mustafa Kemal (later known as Ataturk), did not consider itself bound by treaties signed by the Ottomans. Nor were Kurdish leaders aggressive in their advocacy for independence for their people (McDowall, 1996, *The Kurds*, 4). These factors combined with the fact that Britain had decided to annex parts of central Kurdistan (the vilayet of Mosul and the oil-rich Kurdish district of Kirkuk) to their British Mandate of Iraq sealed the fate of those short-lived hopes for independence (Izady 1992, 60–61). Soon after the Treaty of Sevre, both Turkey and Britain were looking warily at any independence in the Anatolian region of northern Kurdistan. And, in 1923, a new treaty, the Treaty of Lausanne, was signed in which there was no mention of the Kurds or Kurdistan. With this new domination, new and oppressive laws came into place, and there began a series of uprisings in the Kurdish territories that has continued to this day. One of these resulted in the establishment of the first Kurdish republic at Mahabad in Iranian Kurdistan in 1946. However, it was able to survive for only one year. All of the other uprisings were put down with brutality. The revolts often provided those in power with a convenient excuse to ruthlessly burn villages and depopulate whole areas.

Geography

Kurdistan stretches from Kermanshah (Kirmaşan), southwestern Iran; arcing through Mount Ararat (Agirî Mountain), Erzincan, and Adana on the Mediterranean in Turkey; down through Kurd Dagh, Jazira and Hasaka in Syria; to Tal Afar, Kirkuk (Kerkûk), and Khanaqin (Xaneqîn) in Iraq, creating a crescent-shaped land mass. The population and boundaries of Kurdistan must have shifted over thousands of years because of demographic and economic changes and shifts in the military balance of power of the neighboring communities (Izady 1992, 2–3).

Forced Assimilation and Human Rights Abuses

Since World War I, the ruling communities in Turkey, Syria, Iraq, and Iran have used many oppressive ways and means to assimilate their Kurdish communities with a view to depriving them of cultural, linguistic, civic, and political rights that might weaken the power of the central government. The regional states are fearful that the Kurds might one day mobilize their political powerbase and announce independence. Turkey is among the states in which pressure on the Kurds to assimilate has been especially strong. As early as the 1920s and 1930s, laws were passed forbidding the Kurds to speak or write in their native tongue or to give their children Kurdish names. Human rights abuses against the Kurds abound even though Turkey is a signatory of the European Convention on Human Rights. "[Turkey's] widespread use of arbitrary arrest and torture, its use of extrajudicial killings by security forces, its barbarous and indiscriminate methods and practices of village evacuation and coercion of people into its village militia force all violate this [European Convention on Human Rights] Convention" (McDowell 1996, *The Kurds*, 19). In Iraq, the treatment of the Kurds by Saddam Hussein amounts to genocide. During the Al Anfal campaign, launched in 1988, an estimated four thousand Kurdish villages were razed and two hundred thousand Kurds were killed. During this time, Saddam cleared the path for his army by using poison gas on entire towns. The most notorious example of this was the gassing of the town of Halabja where more than five thousand civilians died in a single attack (McDowell 1996, *The Kurds*, 26–27). The American occupation of Iraq in 2003 created an important opportunity for the Iraqi Kurds to consolidate their powerbase and demand a large degree of self-rule within a democratic and federal system of government. The neighboring states have made extensive efforts to prevent the Iraqi Kurds from reaching this objective, fearing they might set a precedent for neighboring Kurdish populations to demand autonomy.

Natural Resources and Conclusion

The various ruling communities do not want to lose control over the natural resources of Kurdistan, which parts of their countries lack. The oil of the Kurdish regions in Iraq, Syria, and Turkey provide considerable revenues to the central governments. The waters of the Tigris and Euphrates Rivers, used for domestic and agricultural production purposes, originate from the snow-capped Kurdistan mountains. Rights to the waters of the Tigris and Euphrates are already a source of tension between the neighboring states because of the scarcity of water in the region. Some political analysts assert that the next war in the Middle East will be about water, which is becoming as valuable as oil to the people of the region. For these reasons, it can be expected that the neighboring states will do all in their power to deprive the Kurds of the resources in their own backyard. The resources of Kurdistan have been mined to pay for the development of other parts of Turkey, Syria, Iraq and Iran. The Kurdish regions in these countries are characterized by rampant unemployment, high illiteracy, child mortality, and malnutrition. The Kurdish regions are kept underdeveloped to oblige the Kurdish population to move to larger cities with a view to expediting their assimilation to the dominant ethnic groups. However, the Kurds have resisted moving from their ancestral land en masse and Kurdish political leaders have mobilized their powerbase to demand a degree of self-rule for the Kurds with a view to enjoying equal civil and human rights and reviving the Kurdish language, history, and culture.

References

Cited Sources

Beaudin Saeedpour, Vera. "The Legacy of Saladin." *International Journal of Kurdish Studies* 13, No. 1. New York: Kurdish Library, 1999.

Brisley, Maya. "Chronology." In *When Borders Bleed* by Ed Kashi. New York: Pantheon Books, 1994.

Herodotus. *The Persian Wars*. Translated by George Rawlinson. New York: Random House, 1942. (As of 2004, this text has been available as an e-book from the University of Adelaide Library online: http://etext.library.adelaide.edu.au/h/herodotus/h4/index.html).

Izady, Mehrdad R. *The Kurds: A Concise Handbook*. New York: Crane Russak, 1992.

McDowall, David. *A Modern History of the Kurds,* 3rd ed. London: I.B. Tauris, 2004.

McDowall, David. *The Kurds: Minority Rights Group International Report*. London: Minority Rights Group, 1996.

Other Resources

Ahmed, Mohammed M. A., and Gunter, Michael M. *Evolution of Kurdish Nationalism*. Costa Mesa, CA: Mazda, 2007.

Al-Khalil, Samir. *Republic of Fear: The Inside Story of Saddam's Iraq*. New York: Pantheon Books, 1989.

Barkey, H. J., and Fuller, G. E. *Turkey's Kurdish Question*. Lanham, MD: Rowman & Littlefield, 1997.

Chaliand, G., and Pallis, M. *A People without a Country: The Kurds and Kurdistan*. London: Zed Books, 1993.

Hassanpour, Amir. *Nationalism and Language in Kurdistan, 1918–1985*. San Francisco: Mellen Research University Press, 1992.

Meiselas, Susan. *Kurdistan, in the Shadow of History*. New York: Random House, 1997.

Mojab, Shahrzad. *Women of a Non-state Nation: The Kurds*. Costa Mesa, CA: Mazda, 2001.

Olson, Robert W. *The Emergence of Kurdish Nationalism and the Sheikh Said Rebellion, 1880–1925*. Austin: University of Texas Press, 1989.

O'Shea, Maria, T. *Trapped between the Map and Reality: Geography and Perceptions of Kurdistan*. New York & London: Routledge, 2004.

Randal, Jonathan, C. *After Such Knowledge, What Forgiveness? My Encounters with Kurdistan*. Boulder, CO: Westview Press, 1999.

Van Bruinessen, Martin. *Agha, Shaikh and State: The Social and Political Structures of Kurdistan*. London: Zed Books, 1992.

Wahlbeck, Osten. *Kurdish Diasporas: A Comparative Study of Kurdish Refugee Communities*. New York: St. Martin's Press, 1999.

Web Sites of Interest

www.akakurdistan.com: Susan Meiselas, author of *Kurdistan, in the Shadow of History*, created this Web site. It features an open forum to share stories and photos of Kurdistan. This fascinating Web site contains poignant and unusual personal tales.

www.kdlib.org: This database allows researchers to search easily for books and journal items related to Kurdish topics.

www.kurdishmedia.com: Here it is possible to find current-event articles on Kurdish topics from journals and newspapers worldwide. Updated daily, this site also features contributions from prominent writers on Kurdish topics. These editorials are helpful for gaining insight into the Kurdish perspective on current events.

www.kurdistanica.com: This site, "The Encyclopedia of Kurdistan," proves a good source of general information about the people and the region. Currently there are many parts still under construction.

www.legoorin.com/muzika_kurdi.php: A Web site where you can hear a variety of Kurdish musicians and singers.

www.legoorin.com/video.php: These Kurdish music videos highlight the people and the landscape, as well as music and traditional dances.

Kurdistan
in the context of the
Middle East

Majority Kurdish
region circa 1992

Outline of map of
Kurdistan submitted to
the San Francisco
Conference of the U.N.
on March 30, 1945

Modern state boundaries

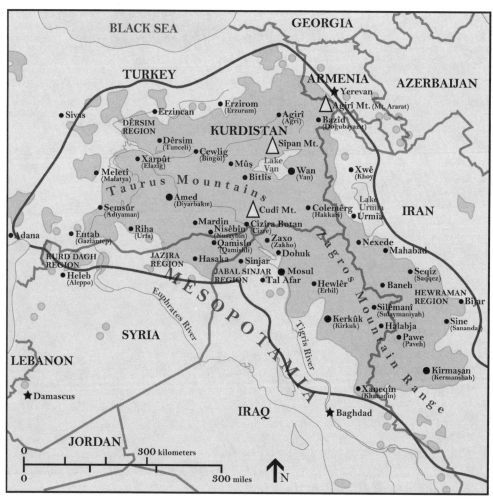

BLACK SEA   GEORGIA

TURKEY   ARMENIA   AZERBAIJAN
                    ★Yerevan

•Sivas   •Erzincan   •Erzirom   △ Agirî Mt. (Mt. Ararat)
                        (Erzurum) •Agirî   •Bazîd
                                    (Agri)   (Doğubayazıt)
            DÊRSIM   KURDISTAN
            REGION
            •Dêrsim   △ Sîpan Mt.
            (Tunceli) •Cewlig
            •Xarpût (Bingöl) •Mûş   Lake
            (Elazig)   Van •Wan   •Xwê
        •Meletî   •Bitlîs   (Van)   (Khoy
        (Malatya)   T a u r u s   M o u n t a i n s   Lake
                                                            Urmi
        •Semsûr   •Amed   △ Cudî Mt. •Colemêrg   •Urmia   IRAN
        (Adiyaman)   (Diyarbakır)   (Hakkari)
    •Adana •Entab •Riha •Mardin •Cizîra Botan   •Nexede
            (Gaziantep) (Urfa) •Nisêbîn (Cizre)   •Mahabad
    KURD DAGH   (Nusaybin) •Zaxo
    REGION   JAZIRA •Qamislo (Zakho)
    •Heleb   REGION (Qamishli) •Dohuk   •Seqîz
    (Aleppo)   •Hasaka •Sinjar   •Baneh   (Saqqez)
                  JABAL SINJAR •Mosul   HEWRAMAN
                  REGION •Tal Afar •Hewlêr   REGION   •Bijar
            SYRIA   (Erbil)   •Silêmanî   •Sine
                                                (Sulaymaniyah)   (Sanandaj)
                                          •Kerkûk •Halabja
        Euphrates River   (Kirkuk) •Pawe
    LEBANON   M E S O P O T A M I A   (Paveh)
                                    Tigris River
        ★Damascus   •Kirmaşan
                                                     (Kermanshah)
                        IRAQ   •Xaneqîn
                                    (Khanaqin)
            JORDAN   ★ Baghdad

    0   300 kilometers
    0   300 miles   ↑ N

Mêvanê yekî mêvanê gundekî.

A guest of one is a guest of the village.

—**Kurdish Proverb**

Recipes

A warm welcome, May 2006. Photo by the author.

XÊR HATIN: WELCOME!

Xêr Hatin (khayr hah-tihn), is the hearty greeting you hear upon entering a Kurdish household. Kurdish hospitality is legendary. Perhaps it is because of life as it is lived in remote mountain villages. Visitors can be rare, and when they arrive, they have often traveled for long distances. The utmost care and compassion, along with the best of everything, is given to the guest. Thick mattresses filled with soft sheep's wool ensure the comfort of weary travelers. So important is the virtue of generous hospitality that it may be a week before the guest is even asked the purpose of the visit.

Kurdish meals are traditionally eaten seated on the floor around a colorful cloth brought out for these occasions. A large bowl in the center holds the meal, and everyone shares from the same bowl. In more recent times, the meal is served family style with every-

one filling their plates with the various foods. In some households or on some occasions, men and women eat separately.

Kurdish foods are similar to those found in many other Middle Eastern cultures. It is quite easy to find the specialized ingredients called for in the following recipes at either a Middle Eastern market or an online source that specializes in products from that part of the world. Other ingredients, for instance goat's milk and goat's milk yogurt should be looked for in health food and natural food stores. Throughout the recipe section, goat's milk or goat's milk yogurt is called for when its distinctive flavor will add an important element to a particular dish or recipe. However, if goat's milk products are not available, full-fat cow's milk or cow's milk yogurt may always be substituted. When hot pepper is called for in the recipes, what is referred to is "crushed red pepper" not "ground red pepper." This is easily found in Middle Eastern markets labeled as "Aleppo red pepper" or simply "crushed red pepper." The rich color and distinctive taste of this kind of red pepper is well worth the trip!

Breakfast

The day begins with a hearty breakfast of hot tea, boiled eggs, and jam or honey of the region, yogurt cream, cucumbers, tomatoes, olives, onions, and either goat's milk or sheep's milk cheese flavored with mountain plants and grasses. The cheese is often covered in salt and left in the ground for a year to cure and preserve it. Several pieces of the large flat bread called lavshe (lahv-sheh), baked in a tandoor oven (Kurdish tandoors are either deep lined pits in the ground or are raised above ground), are given to everyone. It is quite a pleasure to roll up various combinations of ingredients inside of it. One delicious combination is salty mountain cheese and fresh walnuts. A sweeter treat can be the walnut and honey spread gurcebez (guhr-jeh-behz).

Gurcebez: A Walnut and Honey Spread

Walnut trees are abundant and very old in many parts of Kurdistan. Quite a few recipes feature walnuts.

Here, two loaves of kade (kah-deh), a small bread filled with crushed walnuts and honey, are shown atop a large piece of lavshe. (Lavshe is also referred to as nanê tendurê or tandoor bread.) Lavshe is baked in the tandoor in enough quantity to last for several days. Traditionally made from ground wheat, lavshe has a fragrance that is delicately sweet and fresh.

Ingredients:

Walnuts

Fresh local honey

Directions:

Break up the fresh walnuts into pieces about ⅛ inch in diameter. Combine them with enough honey to bind them and give them the consistency of a spread. Serve gurcebez with bread. If you do not have a tandoor oven nearby for lavshe, you can substitute with the lavash bread found at many Middle Eastern markets.

Great herders, the Kurds have an abundance of unusual and tasty milk products in their diet. Jajî, a soft cheese made in the Colemêrg region, from dried goat's or sheep's milk yogurt is just one of these foods. The mountain plants used to create jajî are called birik, siyabû and mendê. These indigenous plants with their strong, sharp tastes are reported to have healing properties. Jajî is pictured in the photo above (left) alongside "Goat's Ears," one of the many mountain plants that lend an unusual flavor to Kurdish foods. The earthy taste and chewy texture of this plant is delightful in the yogurt and hulled wheat soup in which it is traditionally served.

Jajî: A Yogurt Cheese Spread

It isn't possible to make jajî exactly as it would be made in Kurdistan, because there it is flavored with mountain plants unique to the region. But it can be a delicious treat to prepare a "dried" yogurt cheese spread and mix in locally available herbs and plants to enhance the flavor.

Step One: Making the Yogurt

Ingredients:

2 quarts of goat's milk or cow's milk: whole or 2% milk plus

¼ cup of plain whole milk yogurt from goat's or cow's milk or 2½ tablespoons of active yogurt starter

Directions:

Heat 2 quarts of milk until it is so hot that it begins to rise (approximately 180 degrees F, 82 degrees C; a candy thermometer will give an accurate temperature). Do not bring the milk to a complete boil, but keep it at approximately 180 degrees for 5 minutes. Cool slightly and then ladle into a large bowl.

After approximately 10 minutes, when the milk is close to 115 degrees F, place ¼ cup of full-fat plain yogurt in a separate bowl and mix in an equal amount of the warm milk. Pour this mixture back into the heated milk, stirring briefly until it is dissolved. (If you are using yogurt starter, begin by putting 6 tablespoons of the warm milk and the starter powder in a large heavy bowl and make a liquid paste. Continue to add warm milk cup by cup to this paste, stirring until all of the milk is added.)

Once the yogurt (or starter) has been integrated, cover the container so that it is protected from air. Wrap it in towels and place it in a warm location. Let it set for 6–8 hours, preferably not longer than 8 hours (the longer the yogurt sets the more sour it becomes). Do not move or shake the yogurt while it is forming. The yogurt is ready when it has a custard-like consistency.

Refrigerate for at least 7 hours before eating. (Note: In parts of Kurdistan, if the time of year meant that there was no yogurt culture left, dried apricots were used as a starter culture for the yogurt.)

To create yogurt cream, a breakfast delicacy, make the yogurt with a combination of milk and cream. The yogurt cream will be at the top of the yogurt. This is a special treat reserved for guests or for a family member who has been away for a long time.

Step Two: Making Soft Yogurt Cheese

Ingredients:

1 quart of goat's milk or cow's milk yogurt (1 quart of yogurt will yield 1½ cups of soft cheese)

Herbs and plants for flavoring (5 heaping tablespoons of flavorful fresh herbs such as dill, marjoram, or savory for every ¾ cup of soft cheese; approximately 3–4 tablespoons dried celery may be added as well)

½ teaspoon of salt (scant) or less for every ¾ cup of cheese

Directions:

To "dry" your yogurt, line the inside of a fine mesh strainer with three layers of high quality cheesecloth. Cover loosely and place an empty bowl underneath to catch the liquid whey that will drain off. Place the yogurt in the cheesecloth and strain in the refrigerator for two full days. After one day, gently turn the yogurt so that the solids on the bottom do not stop the wetter yogurt on the top from draining further.

Find and prepare local herbs to flavor the soft yogurt cheese. Some good choices include dried pieces of celery (roughly chop into pieces ¼ inch in diameter—dry for 1½ days), chives, dill (chopped roughly—include some stems), marjoram, savory or other strong tasting herbs or greens. (Do not use dried spices or dried herbs in jars.)

Choose two herbs to combine and add to your cheese. (Marjoram and savory should not be used together.) Chop the chosen greens roughly into small pieces. Mix well the plants, yogurt, cheese, and salt.

Wrap the flavored cheese in three layers of cheesecloth and suspend in a cool place for 6 hours to remove any remaining liquid whey. Unwrap and put the soft cheese in a serving or storage container. It will be ready to serve in a few days, once the herbs have infused it with flavor.

Lunch

Lunch is often the heaviest meal, giving energy and sustenance for the rest of the day. If the men are not able to come home, they take a hearty meal with them, or the women cook lunch and bring it to where they are working. On weekends and holidays, lunch can be a family picnic out in the open air. Every kind of vegetable and meat is used and the barbeque can go on for several hours as different foods are cooked in sequence over the grill.

Kifte Gosht: Ground Meat Patties

Ingredients:

1½ pounds ground beef
¾ of a 6-ounce can of tomato paste
½ bunch of flat-leaf parsley (minced very fine)
1 medium red onion (minced so fine that it gives off liquid)
¼ cup extra-virgin olive oil
1 tablespoon turmeric
1½ teaspoons ground cumin
1½ teaspoons crushed red pepper
¾ teaspoon salt and ¾ teaspoon black pepper to taste

Directions:

Place all ingredients in a large bowl. Knead together well. Check for a moist consistency that sticks together. Add more olive oil if necessary. Refrigerate meat in order to cool it if it begins to fall apart.

Prepare the grill. Create 3 inch-wide meat patties. (The meat mixture can also be used as a kebab, formed into thin oblong patties, about 5 inches long, and molded around skewers.) Grill over hot coals basting with additional olive oil until done. (If necessary, the meat patties can be cooked in a fry pan.) Serve with eggplant-pepper side dish. Serves 4–6.

Eggplant-Pepper Side Dish

This dish works best when the vegetables are roasted on a hot grill. If that is not possible, the second recipe, "Eggplant Side Dish Variation," allows for stovetop cooking.

Ingredients:

4 slender Italian eggplants

3 fresh peppers of different sizes and colors (can be a combination of sweet and hot peppers)

1 head of garlic

1 tablespoon extra-virgin olive oil

Yogurt (optional)

Salt to taste

Directions:

Cook eggplants and peppers on top of a hot grill until they are charred and the skin on the peppers begins to peel. Cut off the top of the garlic, revealing the very tip of the individual cloves underneath. Pour a little olive oil onto the top of the head of garlic and in among the cloves. Roast the garlic on top of the grill until it is soft and golden. (Alternatively, the head of garlic can be wrapped in foil and placed among the edges of the coals.) When the cloves are soft and golden, pop them out of their casings.

Peel off the charred skin and dice the roasted eggplant and peppers. Mash or dice all ingredients together. If desired, combine with yogurt to cover and then mix together. Serve with grilled meat and bread. Serves 6.

Eggplant Side Dish Variation (an indoor version)

Take several small thin eggplants (Italian) and cut them into slices ¼ inch thick. Fry in olive oil until they are delicately golden. Drain on paper towels. Gently heat mashed or pressed garlic (6 cloves or to taste) in 1 tablespoon of virgin olive oil until slightly golden. Blend with warm yogurt and then spoon this mixture over the eggplant slices. Serve at room temperature as a side dish or as an accompaniment to meat.

Red Onion Salad

This salad is purported to soothe an upset stomach.

Ingredients:

> 2 red onions
>
> Juice of one medium lemon (use only fresh-squeezed lemon juice)
>
> 1 teaspoon salt
>
> ½ teaspoon crushed red pepper (available at Middle Eastern markets)
>
> 1 lemon cut into wedges
>
> 2 tablespoons finely chopped parsley

Directions:

> Remove the skin from the red onions. Quarter and slice them thinly crosswise. Combine lemon juice, salt, and red pepper and blend well. Drizzle over sliced red onions. Toss well, let sit for 1 hour, and serve. For garnish use lemon wedges and finely chopped parsley. Serves 4–6.

Selete—Simple Salad

Ingredients:

> 2 tomatoes roughly chopped
>
> 1 cucumber roughly chopped
>
> ¼ bunch flat-leaf parsley roughly chopped
>
> 4 green scallions washed and sliced
>
> ¼ cup extra-virgin olive oil
>
> Juice from ½ lemon
>
> ½ teaspoon salt
>
> Black pepper

Directions:

Combine tomatoes, cucumber, parsley, and scallions in a salad bowl. Place olive oil, fresh lemon juice, and salt in a sealed container. Shake until well blended. Pour over the salad. Put fresh ground black pepper to taste, toss, and serve. Serves 4.

Roadside Treats: "Banana of the Mountain," 2006. Photo by the author.

If you are in the Kurdish region of Turkey in May, on your way to or from your picnic, you may see people by the side of the road selling rîvas or rûbês, the flowering center of the rhubarb plant. Strong-tasting foods are a favorite in the Kurdish region and tirş (tihrsh) or sour foods like these are greatly valued not only for their taste but also as a spring tonic. The outer skin of this stalk is peeled back like a banana, and the center is eaten raw. Some mitigate the sourness by dusting the tart inner core with various kinds of sugar.

Breads

Zerfet: An Unleavened Bread Bowl

Ingredients:

3¾ cups bread flour (3 cups white flour, ¾ cup whole wheat flour)

¾ tablespoon salt

1¾ cups water

2 pressed cloves garlic

1½ cups yogurt

4 tablespoons ice water

¼ cup butter

Directions:

Combine flour and salt in a large bowl and mix together. Add water ¼ cup at a time, mixing and kneading by hand each time more water is added. Once 1 cup of water has been integrated, add the water a little at a time. Keeping the dough in the bowl, knead vigorously each time the water is added. The bowl can be stabilized with one hand while the other hand kneads the dough. Initially when the water is added, the dough will be slippery, but as the flour absorbs the water, the dough will become stickier.

When the dough begins to stick so much to the hands that it becomes difficult to knead it, add additional water and knead until the dough becomes sticky again. Continue until approximately 1¾ cups of water have been added and the dough seems unable to easily absorb more water. Let the dough rest for 10 minutes while preheating the oven to 475 degrees F (250 degrees C). Just before baking, knead the dough for four additional minutes, wetting hands as needed to keep the dough from sticking.

With wet hands, place your bread dough into a greased cast iron fry pan (preferred) or a 9-inch pie pan. Mold the bread into a 1-inch-thick round. (If a piece of the dough breaks off from the circle while you are making it, the Kurdish saying is that this means a guest is coming!) The dough will be somewhat loose and difficult to manage. Bake the zerfet round for half an hour. (This recipe has been adapted to cook in a regular oven.) Turn oven heat down to 450 degrees and cook for an additional half hour.

While the zerfet is cooking, make a light yogurt sauce by combining the yogurt with 4 tablespoons of icy cold water and mixing vigorously and well (use a whisk). Combine the garlic with the yogurt mixture. Set aside.

Remove the zerfet from the oven. It should be a rich brown color, hard on the outside and hollow sounding when thumped. Carefully cut a circle around the inside of the top crust ¾ inch from the edge. Score bite-sized squares through this circle shape. The scoring should reach to, but not through, the bottom crust. Remove these scored pieces along with all of the soft dough from the inside of the loaf, leaving a bread shell.

Brush the interior of the bread shell with a layer of the yogurt/garlic combination. Tear all of the bread pieces into bite-sized pieces. Place them back into the bread shell and drizzle the yogurt sauce in a thick circle around the inside and all over, although not in the very center of the bread pile.

Melt ¼ cup of butter. Drizzle the melted butter into the very center of the bread mound and serve immediately. Zerfet is traditionally eaten with the hands. It can stand alone as a hearty meal. It should be eaten as soon as it is cool enough to handle. Serves 2–4.

Bicik: A Dense Bread

Ingredients:

4 cups flour (soft bread flour used for bread machines)
1 teaspoon salt
1 package dry rapid rise yeast (2 teaspoons)
2 eggs
1 cup milk
½ stick melted butter

Directions:

Making sure all ingredients for bicik (bih-jihk) are at room temperature, combine flour, and salt and mix well. Add yeast, eggs, and milk and mix well by hand. Melt butter, let cool slightly and pour into your dough mixture. Knead until integrated and then continue kneading for another 10 minutes until it becomes a firm dough. Form into a fairly flat, smooth round.

Grease a deep-dish pie pan (a glass pie pan works well), and place the dough in it. Gently spread the dough so that it is covers the whole bottom of the pie pan. Brush the top of the dough lightly with beaten egg whites and sprinkle sesame seeds on the top. Cover, put in a warm place, and let rise for two hours.

Place risen bread dough in an oven preheated to 325 degrees F (160 degrees C) and cook for 30 minutes. (Bicik is traditionally cooked under a large metal bowl. The bowl is placed upside down on top of the bicik dough and wood is burned on top. Here the recipe has been adapted for a regular oven.) Remove the bread and turn oven heat up to 425 degrees F (220 degrees C). When that temperature is reached, put the bread back in for five minutes or until it has a golden crust. Bicik is eaten as a simple meal with either tea (çay) or dew (see beverage recipes on pages 24–26). Serves 4.

Evening Meals: Wintertime Stews and More

Large stewpot on the fire, 2006. Photo by the author.

Keledosh: A Vegetarian Stew

This hearty dish is eaten in winter. It is a very rich vegetarian dish.

Ingredients:

¼ cup whole dried chickpeas (or ⅔ cup of canned chickpeas drained and rinsed)

¼ cup dried white beans (or ⅔ cup of canned white beans, cannellini or great northern, drained and rinsed)

¼ cup dried green lentils

½ cup hulled wheat (available at Middle Eastern markets)

2 potatoes (good-sized red potatoes, peeled and cut into large squares)

4 cups whole milk yogurt

2 cloves pressed garlic or more to taste

2 quarts loosely packed hearty greens: in Kurdistan the mountain plants çorîn, a wild mountain herb, and loshe, a wild mountain plant, would be used. But because they are unavailable outside of the regions where this dish is made, substitute with

two of the following: fresh kale, spinach, Swiss chard, watercress, or other substantive greens cut into thin shreds.

Salt to taste

4 tablespoons sweet butter

1 teaspoon dried oregano or a combination of dried oregano and mint

1 teaspoon crushed red pepper

Directions:

Soak the chickpeas, dried beans, and green lentils the day before. The next morning, empty the water that the beans were soaking in, rinse, and then boil the chickpeas, lentils, and dried beans separately till they are *al dente*. (The green lentils will cook quickly so do not cook them for long.) The hulled wheat or dahn (the Kurdish name for hulled wheat) does not need to be soaked in advance but it must be rinsed thoroughly and boiled for one hour or until it is very soft. (If using canned chickpeas and white beans, simply add them to the cooked green lentils and hulled wheat.)

Peel and cut the potatoes into fairly large cubes (they should retain their integrity in the dish). Put them in a vegetable steamer and steam for ten minutes.

After all the ingredients have been boiled and prepared, put them in a deep saucepan. The chickpeas, beans, and lentils should appear whole. Stabilize the yogurt so that it doesn't separate by beating together one egg white with 1 tablespoon of cornstarch and mixing into the cool yogurt. Gently boil the yogurt for several minutes until it begins to thicken. Add the pressed garlic and the plants to the yogurt. Add salt to taste.

Simmer everything together on a low fire. As the plants give off their liquid, the dish will become more watery. As it continues to cook, the dish thickens and becomes more like a stew. When the stew is finished, put it on a large plate. Create a depression in the middle and fill it with melted butter. Serve with bread. Serves 8.

Alternatively, serve the keledosh in individual bowls. Melt 4 tablespoons of butter. Add 1 teaspoon dried oregano or the oregano and mint combination and 1 teaspoon crushed red pepper and cook until they sizzle. Drizzle this mixture over the top of each bowl.

Meleme: A Meat and Egg Dish

Ingredients:

1½ pounds plum tomatoes (approximately 8 plum tomatoes)

4 medium-hot peppers such as Anaheim (if you are using a small, extremely hot pepper, use only one and have the rest be similar to Italian frying peppers, long and thin and sweet. There needs to be enough bulk of peppers for this dish and not over-powering heat).

1 red bell pepper

¾ pound ground beef

¾ tablespoon sunflower or other light oil

Salt to taste

4 eggs, beaten

Crushed red pepper to taste

2 tablespoons minced flat-leaf parsley for garnish

Directions:

Skin and de-seed the tomatoes and cut them into small pieces. To skin the tomatoes, submerge them in boiling water for a minute. Place in a colander, rinse with cool water, then peel off the skins. Cut off the top of the tomato, hold upside down and squeeze to remove the bulk of the seeds. Chop the tomato flesh.

Remove the seeds from the peppers and cut them into small pieces. Sauté meat in the oil with some salt and then add cut peppers. Cook until the peppers are soft. Add tomatoes. Simmer for 15 minutes until the tomatoes are soft and thoroughly cooked. Continue cooking on fairly high heat to evaporate any remaining liquid in the pan.

Add the beaten eggs. Pour lightly over the top. Let the egg mixture reach down to the bottom of the pan by making spaces in the meat, pepper, and tomato mixture. Cover and cook on medium high heat for 5–10 minutes or until the eggs are thoroughly cooked. If necessary, divide the mixture into four sections and turn once to aid in cooking.

Add crushed red pepper to taste or let the guests add it themselves. Serve on individual plates. To garnish, mince parsley and sprinkle on the top. Serve with bread or rice and red onion salad with a side dish of yogurt. Serves 4.

Borinî: A Squash and Lentil Side Dish

Ingredients:

½ cup dried green lentils

1 good-sized butternut squash peeled, de-seeded and cubed

3 garlic cloves

1 cup goat's or cow's milk yogurt

1 teaspoon salt

¼ cup sweet butter

Directions:

Rinse the lentils well and soak overnight. (Note: By adding ¼ cup more dried lentils to the ingredient list, borinî can be eaten alone as a balanced protein vegetarian dish.) Peel and cube the squash. Place in a saucepan. Heat gently on a low fire so that the squash cooks in its own steam until soft. If necessary add water 1 tablespoon at a time so that the squash does not scorch. Rinse lentils well again, bring to a boil and then simmer until tender. Mash the squash.

Press 3 cloves of garlic and add them to the cup of yogurt. Gently bring the yogurt to a boil. (Goat's milk yogurt lends a wonderful flavor to this dish, but if using cow's milk yogurt, stabilize the yogurt first; see instructions for keledosh on pages 13–14.) Add the boiled yogurt mixture to the squash. Add the green lentils and salt.

Ladle into a low bowl. Melt the sweet butter. Create a depression in the middle of the dish and pour butter in it. Serve with bread. Serves 6.

Mehîr: A Cool Yogurt Soup

There are many types of yogurt soup in Kurdistan. This is a simple and simply delicious version.

Ingredients:

1 cup hulled wheat (available at Middle Eastern markets)

½ teaspoon salt

1 quart whole milk yogurt

3 cups room-temperature water

2 cups ice water

Fresh mint for garnish and flavoring

Directions:

Rinse the hulled wheat and put in a pot with salt and three times the amount of water. Bring to a boil and simmer for approximately one hour. Keep adding water as needed. Test to make sure that it has cooked to a nice softness. Rinse well with cool water and set aside. Vigorously mix yogurt together with icy cold water. (Place the water into the freezer and leave there until an ice crust begins to form. Break the crust and use that very cold water for the yogurt/water combination.) Mix the yogurt/water mixture and the cooked hulled wheat together. Before serving, sprinkle finely chopped fresh mint on top of each individual serving. Serves 6.

Red Lentil Soup

Ingredients:

1½ cups very small red lentils (found in Middle Eastern markets)

2½ quarts water or chicken stock

Salt or 2½ tablespoons of vegetable bouillon

¼ stick butter

1 medium sweet or Spanish onion chopped very fine

1 heaping teaspoon crushed red pepper or to taste

2 teaspoons tomato paste

1 lemon cut into wedges

Directions:

Rinse lentils very well by putting them in a sieve and running water over them until the water runs clear. Put them in a deep pot or stovetop casserole dish with 2½ quarts of water and bring to a boil. Thoroughly scald the lentils before reducing the heat to a simmer. Keep stirring continuously so that the lentil puree never clumps on the bottom of the pot or separates out from the water. Remove all of the foam that builds up on the surface of the water while the lentils cook.

Cook until all of the lentils have burst and have reached puree consistency. Add salt to taste. Continue to simmer on low and stir regularly to keep the puree and the water mixed and to keep the puree from sticking to the bottom of the casserole.

Meanwhile, on very low heat, melt butter, add finely chopped onion, and, very slowly, bring the onions to a deep golden color. Make sure not to burn or carmelize the onions. Mix 2 teaspoons hot red pepper flakes into the onions. Add 2 teaspoons tomato paste to deepen the color of the dish, and continue to stir until these elements are integrated with the onions.

Cook one more minute and pour onion mixture into the soup. Deglaze the skillet with a ladle of soup and pour back into the soup so no onion taste is wasted. Taste and adjust seasonings as needed. Let simmer ten more minutes to integrate the flavors.

When serving: provide extra crushed red pepper flakes and wedges of lemon so that the diners can squeeze fresh lemon juice over the soup. Rustic thick-grained bread torn into pieces can be served on the side. This bread can be dropped or dipped into the soup. Serves 8.

Curbecur—Stew

Variations on this dish can be found all over Kurdistan.

Ingredients:

6 lamb chops or the equivalent amount of stew beef

2 tablespoons butter

1 medium onion chopped coarsely into small cubes

5 cloves of garlic cut in half

1½ tablespoons real paprika

3 tablespoons tomato paste

2 zucchini diced into large cubes

3 green and yellow bell peppers chopped into 4–6 pieces

4 small Italian eggplants diced into large cubes (do not peel)

1 tomato chopped into small cubes

3 potatoes peeled and chopped into 4–5 cubes

3 tomatoes sliced into rings (4–5 per tomato) to put on top of stew

Directions:

Remove external fat from 4–6 good-sized lamb chops. Boil meat gently until partially cooked. Place a stovetop stewpot on low heat. Add 2 tablespoons of butter and the chopped onions and garlic. Stir until onions are translucent. Increase the heat and add 1½ tablespoons real paprika and 3 tablespoons of tomato paste. Mix together. Add the lamb and stir to coat.

After 2 minutes, add the zucchini, peppers, and eggplant and mix until the eggplant changes color. Add the chopped tomato and mix all together. After about 4 minutes, add the potatoes and mix everything. When all ingredients change color, add 1 teaspoon of salt and 2½ cups of water (preferably the water used to precook the meat). Do not submerge the ingredients, the water should be half the depth of the ingredients in the cookware. Bring to a boil and cook covered at medium heat for about 10 minutes.

Lift the lid and cover the top of the stew with sliced tomatoes. Decrease the heat by half and cook covered for another 30 minutes or so. Check the water and taste to see if the spices balance each other well. When the eggplant and the peppers are tender, the dish is done. Take off the heat and let rest for 5 minutes. Serve on a large platter or on individual plates. Serves 4 to 6 people. Accompany with rice.

In a variation of this dish, the meat in the dish is chicken (skinless legs and thighs with the bone in). No zucchini or potatoes are used and no tomatoes slices top the dish. Toward the end of the cooking, eggs are cracked into the bubbling stew. The stew is not stirred after this point and the eggs remain whole, served as part of the dish and making an unusual presentation.

Kutilk: A Filled Dumpling

Ingredients for the dumpling shell:

½ pound finely ground bulgar (available at Middle Eastern markets)

½ pound semolina (durum semolina)

Small amount of salt

Water

Ingredients for the filling:

¼ cup sunflower or other light oil

1 pound ground beef

1 pound finely minced onion

Salt, black pepper and crushed red pepper for seasoning

½ bunch finely minced flat-leaf parsley

Directions:

Prepare the paste for the dumpling shell by mixing well the finely ground bulgar, semolina, and 1 teaspoon of salt. Spread on a large tray. Pour room temperature water all over the grains and soak them thoroughly. Let the mixture rest and absorb water for 1 hour or until the grains feel very soft to the touch. If they are not soft, let them soak longer. Drain any excess water and knead well until a thick paste is formed. (Or, instead of kneading, use a food processor as though making pasta.) The paste should be pliable to the touch, not too dense or hard, and not too loose or soft.

Preparing the filling. Chop the onion and parsley medium fine. They should be minced but still have integrity. Warm the oil in a large fry pan. On low heat, cook the meat thoroughly, then add the minced onion and spices. Mix and cook together so that the flavors blend well. The onion should be thoroughly cooked. Add additional oil as needed. At the very end, add the parsley, cook and mix one more minute, and then remove from the heat. (The filling will have cooked for approximately 45 minutes.)

Prepare the dumpling shell. Take some wheat paste, about the size of a walnut, and make it into a firm shape that will fit in the palm of a hand. Cradle the wheat paste in one hand, and with the index finger of the other hand in the center of the paste ball begin to hollow it out. Turning both the finger and the hand as needed to make the walls of the kutilk. Once the walls are evenly thin (the walls will expand when the dumpling is cooked) and there is a hollow inside, place 1 tablespoon of filling inside and close the opening. The kutilk will have a triangular shape. One by one, continue shaping and making the kutilk.

Prepare a big pot of water and keep at a boil on the stovetop. Put 15–20 kutilk into the boiling water at one time. When the kutilk are added, the boiling water will become cooler because the kutilk are cold. When the water comes to a rolling boil again, the kutilk are ready. Remove them from the water and put in the next batch of 15–20 kutilk until they are all cooked. They may be served as is, or they can then be dipped in an egg batter and fried in oil. Serves 6.

Helisa: A Chicken and Wheat Dish

This dish is sometimes served at wedding celebrations.

Ingredients:

1½ pounds hulled wheat (available at Middle Eastern markets)

1 whole chicken skinned and cut into sections. Beef or lamb may also be used but chicken is preferable as it integrates and dissolves better into the dish. (One chicken breast along with two leg and thigh combinations [skinless] can be substituted for the whole chicken.)

Water—enough to cover all ingredients

Salt to taste

Sweet butter

Directions:

Set the hulled wheat to soak overnight. The next day, rinse well and cover with fresh water. Add the skinless chicken cut into parts with enough water to cover and bring to a boil. Stir all together.

Reduce heat to a simmer. Keep adding water as the hulled wheat absorbs it. Stir constantly. Do not leave the pot untended. (If using a large crockpot, cook slowly on high for three hours, adding water and stirring occasionally.)

Keep on a low simmer until the chicken is falling off the bones. Remove the bones of the chicken as they become free from the meat, after three hours or so. Make sure that no tiny bones from the chicken breast remain in the helisa.

Mash your ingredients lightly with a potato masher. At this point, the ingredients will start to merge together. Small pieces of dahn and chicken can be seen, but the whole dish is homogenous. Serve warm on a large platter.

Melt the butter. Make a depression in the middle of the dish, fill with butter and serve with lavshe or thin lavash bread. The bread is used to scoop up the helisa. Serves 12–15.

Variation: To make individual servings, the helisa may be used as the main ingredient of a lavash roll-up adding chopped tomatoes, cut peppers, sliced red onions, flat-leaf parsley and extra salt.

Sweeter Dishes

Xebisa/Heola: A Flour-Based Dessert

Ingredients:

½ cup butter
2 cups flour
½ cup water
½ cup sugar
Optional: ½ cup chopped walnuts or pistachios

Directions:

Melt butter in a heavy skillet that is nonstick and good at conducting heat so that the mixture does not burn easily. Add an equal amount of flour as the butter is rising. Keep heat very low and continue to add flour slowly a few tablespoons at a time until the mixture is pale brown (often referred to as "pink"), the color of light brown sugar. Be careful not to let the flour/butter mixture burn.

After adding flour, stir the mixture until the oil from the butter begins to emerge again. This means the last amount of flour that was added has been integrated into the butter. When the sheen of the butter is seen again, this is called "the butter coming through." After all of the flour has been added, add finely chopped walnuts or pistachios to the butter and flour mixture.

Prepare sugar and water by boiling them together for a few minutes until a simple syrup is formed. Before adding the sugar/water to the flour/butter mixture test it first by taking a small amount of the flour/butter mixture and placing it on a plate. Add a small amount of the sugar/water to it. There should be an airy hissing sound as it is mixed in and the new mixture should stick together well. If it does not stick together when pressed, continue to stir the flour/butter combination adding more flour or butter (if your mixture is too crumbly, add butter; if it is too gummy, add flour) until the mixture is the right consistency and then try adding the sugar/water combination again.

Form into small balls and cool. It should have a texture similar to shortbread. Serves 6–8.

Snow Treats

Kurdistan is deeply covered in snow during the winter months. Pure snow or crushed ice (snow cones) combined with other flavorings was looked on as a delightful treat. Mixes can include snow and mast (yogurt), snow and dims (grape molasses) and snow and hingiv (honey), or a combination.

Bastêq: Dessert Roll-up

In Kurdistan, this slightly sweet fruit paste is sun dried on the flat rooftops of the houses.

Ingredients:

1 cup grape molasses* (available at Middle Eastern markets)
½ cup water
Flour as needed

Directions:

Place 1 cup of grape molasses in a saucepan add ½ cup water and bring to a boil for one minute. (When increasing this recipe, the proportion will always be two parts of grape molasses to one part water.) Remove from the heat. In a separate bowl, place ¾ cup of the heated molasses/water mixture. Whisk in flour until it becomes heavy and dense like warm pudding on the stove. Begin to heat the original molasses/water mixture again and slowly add back in your molasses/flour mixture. Stir constantly being careful not to burn the mixture and boil together for 3–5 minutes until the mixture binds well.

The resulting molasses, flour, and water mixture is called pelul (peh-luhl). To dry it, spread thin 4-inch squares on plastic wrap and place in a food dehydrator to dry. After it is dry enough to maintain its shape without the plastic, remove it from the plastic wrap and continue drying until it feels flexible but leathery to the touch.

Alternatively, the mixture can be poured onto a silicone baking mat, spread thin and dried for 12 hours in a 105–115 degree F oven (45–65 degrees C). (In Kurdistan, pelul (or belul) would be poured onto a clean white cloth and dried in the sun over several days upon the flat roofs of the houses.) After it is dry and stiff like thin leather, cut into 4-inch squares.

Place walnuts inside the dried fruit paste, and roll up the slices to eat. Bastêq is a food that was meant to be stored for later use. It was designed for the long winter months when there was little food. For storage, the individual pieces of bastêq can be wrapped in plastic wrap so that they do not stick to each other and placed in an airtight container.

* In the southern regions of Kurdistan "dims" or "duşav," a sweet grape molasses is made. Yellow grapes are crushed and strained thoroughly so that the juice runs clear. The grape juice is then boiled for a whole day until it becomes syrup. Dims tastes delicately light and sweet like a very thin and light sugarcane molasses. Bastêq or dried fruit roll-ups are traditionally made from boiled grape juice as a base, not grape molasses. But because commercially available grape juice does not yield the right results, the substitution here is to use diluted grape molasses.

Benî: A Sweet Walnut Necklace

Walnuts are strung on a thread to make benî.

Benî (beh-nee) is made in the fall when the grapes are ripe. It is eaten for the rest of the winter and is an important wintertime food. When benî is made in the village, the women collect as many as a thousand walnuts. They are put in a large deep platter called a tesht and soaked in water overnight. The next day, the walnut shell is soft, and it is easy to remove the walnut meat in two halves with no breakage.

Ingredients:

    Walnut halves

    Pelul (see recipe for bastêq pages 22–23)

Directions:

Soak whole walnuts in water overnight. Split them in half, and extract the walnut meat in two halves. (If using preshelled walnut halves, soak them in water for several hours so that they do not shatter when pierced by the needle.) Using a needle and thread, string together the walnut halves. (It is important that the string used is strong enough so that it doesn't break when pulled out of the benî.)

Make a large container of pelul following the recipe directions for bastêq on pages 22–23. Prepare a large amount of pelul in a deep container. When the strung walnuts are ready, dip them into this thick mixture. It sticks to the walnuts creating an outer sheath. Dip the walnut strings once or twice or more, depending on how thick people like the outer covering on their walnuts. After the string of walnuts has been dipped, it is hung to dry. Before serving, the string is pulled out of the walnuts.

Vexwarin—Beverages

Although it did not originate in Kurdistan, çay (black tea) is certainly a drink of choice. A delicate loose black Ceylon tea is prepared in a teapot that has two separate chambers.

Çay—Tea

Ingredients:

    Black Ceylon tea

    Water

Directions:

Place tea grounds in the top chamber of the pot and water in the bottom chamber. Bring water to a boil in the bottom pot. Once the water has boiled and has gently heated the grounds in the top pot, let it set for a few minutes.

Briefly rinse the tea in the top chamber with the hot water and quickly pour out that first tea water. Add enough boiled water to fill the top chamber and refill the bottom chamber with room temperature water.

While the water in the bottom chamber comes to a boil, the tea in the top chamber steeps. After the water in the bottom chamber has boiled for the second time, the teapot is set to rest. When it is served, guests choose how strong or light they would like their tea. To make it stronger, more tea is added from the top chamber, to make it lighter, more water is added from the lower chamber. Sugar is typically served in cubes.

Dew: A Yogurt Drink

Ingredients:

1 cup yogurt

Pinch of salt

1 cup icy cold water

Directions:

Whisk 1 cup of yogurt and a little salt in a bowl. If the yogurt is sweet, put in more salt; if it is too acidic, use less salt. Place the water into the freezer and leave there until an ice crust just begins to form. Break the crust and use that very cold water for the yogurt/ice-water combination. Slowly add the cold water to the yogurt, beating continuously, until it has all been added. Beat the yogurt/ice-water combination vigorously until it becomes thick. The resulting drink is called dew (dahohw). Serves 2.

Xweşav—Good Water

Ingredients:

1 cup of mixed dried fruits of the region, any combination of cherries, apricots, grapes (raisins), and pears. (If the emphasis is on a drink rather than on a soup, dried pears are especially nice.)

6 cups water

Sugar (optional)

Directions:

To make xweşhav (kwahsh-ahv), wash all dried fruits and remove any hard elements from them, especially from apricots and pears. Place the fruit in a deep pot. Cover the dried fruit with 6 times the amount of cold water as the fruit (use 4 times the amount of water if making soup). Bring water to a boil and gently boil for 1 hour. Let the fruit rest in the water for 6–7 hours. If desired, add 1 teaspoon of sugar or to taste. This water should not be thick like the water of stewed prunes; it should be light. The raisins will have lost their color and swollen to the size of chickpeas, and the broth of the soup will be faintly sweet. This gentle drink may be strained or served with the fruit still in it. It should be cool but not freezing cold. It can also be served as a delicious fruit soup. Serves 6.

Noşî Can Be!! (noh-shee jahn bah)—Enjoy!!

Bext nadim bi text.

I wouldn't trade good luck for a throne.

—Kurdish Saying

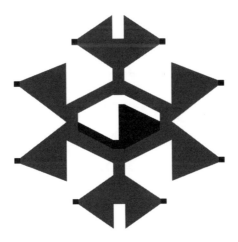

Games!

In Kurdistan there are hundreds of games of skill and dexterity. Most of them can be played with the simple elements we find in nature: sticks, stones, and our own ingenuity.
Wan region, May 2006. Photo by the author.

Gustîlanê: The Ring Game

Gustîlanê (guh-steel-ah-nay) is a wintertime game played by large groups of people.

Pieces

10 walnut shells (To split the walnut easily to get two shells of equal size, it is best to soak the walnuts in water overnight.)

One ring or one sugar cube

Players

This game is for all ages and is played by two teams of equal size.

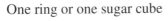

Object of the Game

To get as many points as possible either by guessing the ring's location correctly or by gaining points when the opposing team is unable to guess the location of the ring.

Choosing the Team That Will Go First

(In this game and all of the games that follow, the personal pronoun "he" is used for the sake of convenience to denote either a male or a female player.) Each team chooses a representative to take part in a contest that will determine which team will go first. One of the representatives hides the ring under one of two walnut shells. His opponent tries to guess under which shell the ring has been hidden. If he guesses correctly, then his team gets to hide the ring first. If he does not guess correctly then the other team gets to hide the ring first.

The Game

Ten walnut shells are placed upside down on a great platter. The team that has won the right to hide the ring first (for example, Team A) goes off to the side where they cannot be seen. They strategically hide the ring under one of the shells and return to place the platter in front of Team B. Team B then attempts to discover which shell is hiding the ring. (Note: each member of Team B can take a turn selecting and turning over the walnut shell of their choice, or there can be a designated leader who will do this for the group.)

To score 10 points, Team B must find the shell that the ring is hidden under on the first try. (In some regions, it is a sugar cube that is hidden.) If they think that the ring will be under a certain shell, they point to it saying, "Desta gul," which means "My choice" or "It's my favorite." Then they turn that shell over. If the ring is under that shell, they score 10 points, and it is their turn to hide the ring. But if the ring is not under that walnut shell, then one by one they have to find the shells that are empty until only two are left.

When Team B is selecting a shell that they think has no ring under it, they point to it and say "Pûç" (pooch) which means "empty" or "hollow." Then they turn it over to see if they are right. If they are wrong and the shell that they said was empty does have the ring underneath it, their turn is over, and Team A gets a point for every shell still upside down on the platter. For Team B to succeed with this strategy, they must have all of the walnut halves they turn over be empty until there are only two left.

When there are only two shells left, this a critical moment. Team B now has to find the walnut shell with the ring underneath it on the first try. If they succeed at this, then it is their turn to hide the ring (or the sugar), and Team A does not get any points. If they are wrong, Team A gets one point for the one shell left upside down and also gets to hide the ring again.

Part of the fun of this game is that it lends itself to various approaches as each team tries to find a winning strategy. When Gustîlanê is played in Kurdistan, the team that is trying to discover the location of the ring discusses at great length which shell it might be under. They look to see if they can get any clues from the facial expressions or attitudes of the people on the opposing team. They try to trick them into betraying some information by almost choosing a walnut and then stopping, just to see what the reaction will be. They can employ whatever strategy they want, and they can change it as the game goes along. The discussions and theories about the ring's location can go on for a long time. The team that has hidden the object has to survive whatever questions the opposing team asks and never betray where the object is hidden either by glance of eye or shuffling feet. Usually one or another person cannot help but look at the shell where they have hidden the ring. Even without meaning to, someone's attention will go to that shell. Sometimes the team that has hidden the ring will try to dissemble and fool everyone by sneaking looks at the wrong walnut.

Winning and Losing

The team with the highest score wins. Before the game, the players agree on how many points will be needed to win. The teams also agree on what the penalty will be for the losing team. Sometimes the losing team has to perform some work for the winning team. Sometimes they have to prepare a big meal for them or give them some food. If they lose very badly, they may need to roast a sheep for everyone, but if it is not a huge loss, then they may only have to give the other team a lot of apples or other fruit.

Variations

In Amed, Gustîlanê is played with small cups covering the ring or sugar cube instead of walnut shells. In Nisêbîn, there are no walnut shells used. Everyone on the team that is hiding the ring holds out closed fists, palm side down. One of the team members has the ring hidden in one of his fists. In the Nisêbîn version, if you guess "Desta gul" on the first try, then your team gets 5 points, and the other team loses 5 points.

Bîstberkanê: Sheep and Wolves or Twenty Stones

Bîstberkanê (beest-behr-kah-nay) is a two-person board game.

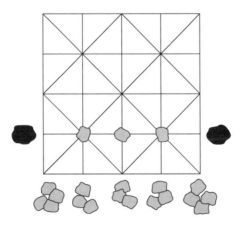

Set up of board and playing pieces for Bîstberkanê.

Pieces

Wolves: two dark stones

Sheep: twenty lighter-colored stones of smaller size

Pattern of the game board can be drawn on a large sheet of paper or traced on the ground as shown. To begin, place pieces in their starting positions as shown in the diagram.

Players

This game is for two players.

Object of the Game

Objective of the Wolves: To "eat" all of the sheep. The sheep are eaten when a wolf piece jumps over a sheep piece to land on an empty line intersection on the other side of it. The wolves can jump over more than one sheep in the same turn (see illustration to right).

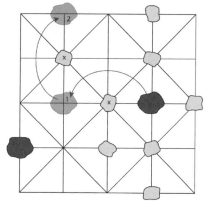

A wolf piece "eats" two sheep.

Objective of the Sheep:

To move all of their playing pieces onto the board and at the same time to block the wolves from jumping over their pieces and "eating" them. A wolf is blocked from moving when sheep pieces are on all consecutive intersections near them preventing them from moving.

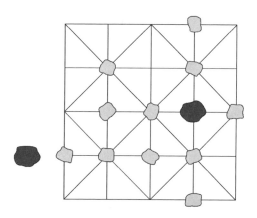

If the sheep succeed in blocking both wolves, they win the game.

The Game

Two dark stones represent the wolves. Their starting position is on either side of the board as shown in the first diagram. The wolves can move one intersection in any direction they want to: up, down, or sideways. Light stones represent the sheep. Their starting position is with seventeen of them off and three on the board as shown in the first diagram on the previous page.

The person representing the sheep gets to move one of his pieces first. The sheep can only move one intersection at a time, but they may move in any direction. They cannot jump over another piece, and there cannot be two sheep or a sheep and a wolf on the same intersection at the same time.

After a sheep piece has been moved to its new position, it is the other player's turn to move one of the wolf pieces onto the board. The person representing the wolves has to choose which wolf piece to use, the one on the right side of the board or the one on the left side of the board. He can only use one of his wolf pieces until all of his opponent's sheep are "out of the pen" (on the board). When all the sheep are out of the pen, the second wolf piece can enter the board. No wolf can enter the board if sheep are blocking its entrance (filling in the entry intersection and the one behind it).

The wolves try to find opportunities to jump over the sheep to "eat them," eliminating from the game the pieces of their opponent that they have jumped over. The sheep can never jump over the wolves, but they can corner them.

Winning and Losing

The game is won when either all of the sheep have been "eaten" and removed from the game or when the two wolves are completely surrounded so that they cannot move.

Pênc Beranê: Five Stones

Pênc Beranê (paynj beh-rah-nay) is a game of skill and dexterity for two or more people. It is typically played by teenagers or young people.

Pieces

Five small stones

Players

There is no limit to the number of players. Players sit in a circle and take their turn one after the other.

Object of the Game

To successfully complete all of the challenges and get the best score in doing so.

Choosing the Person Who Will Go First

Each player takes a turn throwing the five stones up in the air with one hand and trying to catch them on the back of the same hand. Whoever catches the most stones on the back of his hand goes first. If there is a tie, then those two play against each other until one of them catches more stones on the back of his hand than the other.

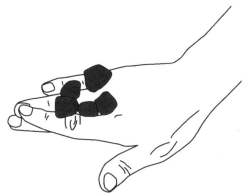

A player succeeds in catching all five stones on the back of the hand.

The Game:

1. First Challenge

The player chosen to go first holds all five stones in one hand. He tosses them up in the air and quickly turns over the same hand to catch the stones on the back of it. (Beginners may need to catch the stones on the backs of both hands instead of just one. In that case, after they toss up the stones, they should quickly turn their hands over, pressing them together at the index fingers with thumbs concealed underneath to allow for as much surface area as possible on which to catch the stones.)

If a player does not catch any stones on the back of his hand, or if he only catches one, he does not score, and that is the end of his turn. However, if the player does catch stones on the back of his hand he then needs to toss them up off of the back of his hand and catch them again in his palm. If he is successful at catching all of those stones, then that number becomes his score for this beginning challenge. If he is not able to catch them all, then this is the end of his turn, and he does not receive any points.

If a player has successfully caught more than one stone on the back of his hand and successfully recaught the same number, he gets to move on to the Second Challenge.

2. Second Challenge

The Second Challenge has five parts to it: yek, du, sê, çar and pênc, which are the Kurdish numbers one, two, three, four and five.

2.1 Yek ~ One

In Yek (yehk) the player spills all of the stones on the floor in front of him. He picks up one of the stones to become his "throwing stone" and tosses it in the air. While that stone is in the air, he must pick up one of the remaining stones in enough time to catch the throwing stone as it descends. (This and the following challenges are all done with one hand.)

The player continues to pick up the three other remaining stones one by one in the same manner. Alternatively, if the player is very good at the game, he can toss his throwing stone into the air and pick up all of the remaining four stones at once before catching the descending stone, in that way completing the Yek challenge. The player will lose his turn if he lets the throwing stone fall to the ground.

It is important to note that for this challenge, and for all of the other challenges, as long as the player catches the throwing stone, he can keep trying to complete the task, and his turn doesn't end.

2.2 Du

Everything is the same, except in Du (duh) the player must pick up the stones in units of two, picking up two stones at a time or, alternatively, four at once.

2.3 Sê

In Sê (say), the player's challenge is to pick up three stones at once and then one stone.

2.4 Çar

In Çar (chahr), the player must pick up all four stones in one swoop while the throwing stone is in the air.

2.5 Pênc

In Pênc (paynj) with the four stones in his hand from completing Çar, the player again tosses his throwing stone into the air. While it is in the air, he brushes the empty ground with the same hand to indicate there are no stones left to pick up. Then he catches the descending stone.

3. Third Challenge: Qafik

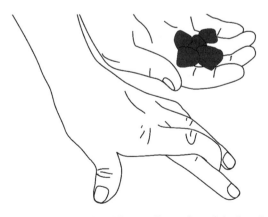

Qafik is the bridgelike configuration of the hand.

The player creates a bridgelike configuration with his left hand (this is assuming that the player is right-handed; left-handed players use the right hand. The bridge is created by crossing index finger over middle finger and then stretching the thumb and middle finger apart, creating a wide bridgelike space between the thumb and middle finger as it rests upon the ground. The ring finger and pinky can be in the air.

The player then takes the stones in his right hand and, crossing the right hand underneath the left wrist, tosses the stones over the back of the Qafik hand toward the right. Whatever configuration the stones land in will be the configuration he has to play for this last challenge. One by one, the player will need to pass the stones under the Qafik "bridge."

The other players get to choose the "last stone," the stone that will be the last one the player must pass under the bridge of his hand. To make the work difficult, they may choose a "last stone" that is in-between the hand bridge and another stone. The rule is that the player must not touch or move the "last stone" with his hand or with any other stone or his turn will be finished.

After the other players have chosen the "last stone," the player then gets to choose one of the other stones on the ground to be his "throwing stone." While the throwing stone is in the air, he must pass the other stones one by one underneath his hand bridge by quickly brushing them in that direction. The player gets as many turns as necessary to move the stones under the hand bridge, as long as he does not drop his throwing stone. He can take several turns to move a stone gradually under the bridge, except for the "last stone." The last stone needs to be moved under the bridge with one sweep.

As long as the player does not drop the throwing stone, he can continue to play and try to move the stones under the Qafik bridge. However, if he drops the throwing stone, or touches the last stone either with his hand or with the stone he is moving, he loses his turn. When his turn comes around again, he has to begin with the challenge of Qafik again.

Winning and Losing

Highest score wins. Players can play a number of rounds or they can play until someone reaches a previously agreed on score, say 20 or 50 points. There are no points gained for the Second or Third Challenge but these challenges must be completed in order to repeat the First Challenge again and score points.

How and Why Legends of Nature

Dinya dem e, salek şûv e, salek lem e.

Life has seasons, some years giving fruit, some years fallow.

—Kurdish Proverb

Mount Ararat, 2005. Photo courtesy of Tom Megan.

Stories of Mountains

Big Ararat and Little Ararat

At 16,854 feet, Çiyayê Agirî (chee-yah-yay ah-gihr-ee) or Mount Ararat,[1] located in northeastern Turkey, towers above the little town of Bazîd (Doğubayazit). The height of Mount Ararat, its legends, and its personality have made it famous all over the world. For generations, Kurds have guided visitors to the top. Many tourists travel to see Ararat because it is said that this is the mountain where Noah's ark came to rest after the flood. In fact, local Kurdish guides say that at the top of this special mountain double rainbows can often be seen. At the summit of Mount Ararat, there is always a cap of snow with icy glaciers underneath. Çiyayê Agirî Bicuk (chee-yah-yay ah-gihr-ee bih-jook) or Little Ararat, the small mountain nearby, is reported to have dangerous creatures on it. Old folktales tell us the reason for this.

*A*ccording to legend, there once lived two sisters who were forever fighting with one another. Day and night they argued, and they always had mean and spiteful words to say. Everyone in the family began to hate their quarreling, and at last the mother of the girls could stand it no longer. To the eldest she said, "You have no warmth toward your sister. Because of this, I pray that Xwedê (kweh-day)[2] will cause your head to be forever encased in ice and snow." She also cursed the younger of the two sisters saying, "Because of your spiteful ways, I pray that you will always have hateful creatures—snakes, wolves, and scorpions—crawling upon you."

Xwedê heeded the mother's request and turned those two girls into mountains. The oldest daughter is the larger mountain, Big Ararat (Mount Ararat), and on its summit there is always snow and ice. But her younger sister became Little Ararat, and to this day that small mountain has many foxes, snakes, and other wild creatures roaming across it.

Notes: Collected in May 2005 from a fifty-six-year-old shepherd, Agirî (Mount Ararat) region, Kurmancî.

1. The Kurds call Mount Ararat Çiyayê Agirî meaning "Crying Mountain" or "Mountain of Fire."

2. Xwedê means God.

Stories of the Night Sky

Why Sun Goes by Day and Moon Goes by Night

*I*n those days, the sun was a girl and the moon was a boy. The sun-girl said to her moon-brother, "I'm afraid to go out walking when it is night." "Don't worry," he said, "I will walk during the night so that you can walk during the day."

Note: Collected in May 2005 from a fifty-five-year-old woman, Bitlîs region, Kurmancî.

Rîya Kadiz:
The Ḫay Thief's Road

In Kurdistan, it is very important to have food for your cattle or sheep during the winter months. The animals can starve to death if there is not enough stored hay because of a drought the summer before or if the winter has been particularly long or severe. Therefore, to steal the fodder reserved for another man's animals can be a very serious crime. In this tale, a man steals "ka"(kah) from another man. Ka is fodder for the animals—ground-up wheat once the grain has been removed or ground-up straw or hay. For convenience's sake, in this story, we call ka: ground-up hay or fodder. Kadiz means "hay thief" and rîya means road.

One evening, a man set out to steal some fodder from another man. Of course he didn't want to be discovered, but, as he was returning home, his arms were so full that little pieces kept falling from his grasp. They slipped out of his arms or the wind teased them away. When he arrived at his door, he turned and looked back. "Oh no," he said. "My tail is as smooth as a fox's!"—that is to say, "I am in big trouble!" Starting at his door and all the way back to the place from which he had stolen the fodder there was a wide trail of bits and pieces of hay.

The man was beside himself with worry. It would be obvious to everyone that he had stolen the fodder; he had scattered bits of it right to his very own door. Out of fear and anxiety he prayed to God. "Xwedê (kweh-day)," he said, "Please take me up into the sky. I don't want to be punished. I don't want anyone to discover that it was I who stole the hay." Xwedê answered the man's plea and raised him up into the sky. But Xwedê did not just lift up the man. No! The whole trail, the record of what he had done, was raised up along with him.

And so, every evening when the sun sets, that man passes across the sky carrying the fodder that he took and leaving a trail of bits and pieces behind him. That is why the Kurdish name for the Milky Way is "Rîya Kadiz" (ree-yah kah-dihz) or the "Hay Thief's Road." Every night you can see the pathway. That thick road of stars is the telltale sign of what he did.

Note: Collected in May 2005 from an eighty-one-year-old man, Bitlîs region, Kurmancî.

Why the Moon Has Dark Spots

**A pure and fresh kanî (spring) gushes from the side
of a rocky cliff, 2006. Photo by the author.**

*The Kurdish region abounds in fresh, clean waters that spring from the rocks and
mountainsides. It is always a pleasure to drink from these very delicious springs called kanî
(kah-nee). It is said that some kanî are so freezing cold, if you place a whole watermelon on
top of them, the watermelon will crack.*

*T*here once lived a girl who was so beautiful she shone with light. Her name was
Heyv (hayv), and she was a shining girl.

One day her mother was making dough to bake bread in the tandoor. She mixed together flour, water, salt, and fermented yeast, but then she realized that her dough was going

to be too dry. She had no more water left to moisten it, so she sent her daughter to the kanî to fetch some water.

As the girl walked to the kanî, everyone stopped to stare at her. She was so beautiful. Heyv was surprised that everyone was looking at her and asked, "Why is everyone looking at me?" She didn't even know how beautiful she was. Everyone wanted to stop her and talk to her and so she was very late returning with the water.

When Heyv returned home, her mother was waiting for her with her hands still covered with the dry and sticky dough. Her mother was so angry with her for coming back so late, that she reached out her fingertips and stuck dough all over her daughter's face.

Heyv prayed to Xwedê (kweh-day) to take her away from this place. Xwedê heard her plea and she vanished right before her mother's eyes. She became the moon. That is why there are all those dirty spots on the face of the moon. That is the dough from her mother's hands.

Note: Collected in May 2005 from a fifty-five-year-old woman, Bitlîs region, Kurmancî.

Stories of Birds and Animals

Pepûk: The Origin of the Cuckoo

A woman gathers mountain plants. On her back is a traditional
carrying sack, 2006. Photo by the author.

During the warmer months, the Kurdish people go to the mountains to gather herbs and plants. These unusual mountain plants give distinctive flavors to their stews and cheeses. In this story, a boy and a girl gather kengir (kehn-gihr), a type of wild artichoke.

*O*nce there lived a brother and a sister. One day, their stepmother sent them up into the mountains to collect kengir, a wild artichoke. The stepmother wanted them to be gone for a long time, so she gave them a large sack to fill. As they walked along, the girl cut off the kengir with her knife, and then she passed the vegetable to her brother to put into the sack. They worked for hours but, because there was a hole in the sack, the kengir

---

always fell out and the sack remained empty. Time after time the girl would ask her brother if the sack was full, and time after time her brother would say no.

From morning till evening they gathered and at last the girl asked her brother to show her how much kengir was in the sack. She looked in and found out that the sack was completely empty. She was very upset with her brother. She knew that their stepmother would be furious with them for collecting all day long and coming home with nothing.

"What did you do with the kengir?" the girl asked.

"I didn't do anything," said her brother.

"I think you ate them all!"

He denied eating any saying, "If you don't trust me, cut me open with your knife. You will see that I have nothing in my stomach."

The girl was very angry and acting crazy. She said, "I am going to look in your stomach." But when she cut open his stomach, she found that it was empty. Now her brother was dead, and she was filled with regret. She walked away in shock realizing that she had just killed the brother she loved.

As she walked, she saw kengir lying all along the path. Then she knew that the reason they had not been able to collect any was because their sack had a hole in it. She was so heartbroken that she began to cry, "Wêêêê, pepû kekû!" (wee peh-poo keh-koo)—which means, "Poor me, I am so miserable."[1] She continued to cry day and night over what she had done.

She prayed to Xwedê (kweh-day), "As my punishment, I beg you, turn me into a bird. Then I will cry and lament for generations to come." Xwedê turned her into pepûk (peh-pook), a cuckoo,[2] and she flew off into the mountains. To this day, pepûk sings this song:

"Pepû! Kekû!" (peh-poo keh-koo)—"Poor me! Poor me!"

"Kî kuşt? Min kuşt." (kee kusht mihn kuhst)—"Who killed? I killed."

"Kî şuşt? Min şuşt."(kee shusht mihn shusht)—"Who washed? I washed."[3]

"Kî hilanî? Min hilanî." (kee hih-lah-nee mihn hih-lah-nee)—"Who buried? I buried."

The Kurdish people know that the mystery of this bird is that it is really a girl forever filled with sorrow and lament because she killed her brother.

Notes: Collected between 2002 and 2006 from various Kurdish tellers: Cafer Sahin, Gulcem Aktas, and others, Dimilî and Kurmancî.

1.   Pepûk means poor, miserable, and weak, it is also the Kurdish name for the cuckoo.

2.   The cuckoo, or pepûk as it is called in Kurdistan, features very strongly in Kurdish culture. It is considered to be a bird of bad omen that brings and feeds on destruction. Pepûk frequents areas where there has been a fire. "Pepûk now sings in our village," became a phrase the Kurdish people used to indicate that their village had been burned down and destroyed.

3.   In Kurdistan, the dead are washed before burial.

How the Owl Came to Be

*O*nce there lived a stepmother and her two stepchildren, a boy and a girl. The stepmother was always cruel to them. She made them work day and night, and she always found fault with what they did. One of their jobs was to watch the sheep, taking them up into the mountains to graze. One day, as they were taking the flock back down the mountain, they lost one of the lambs. Their stepmother was so angry with them. Even though night was coming on, she sent them out to search for it. They looked and looked for the little lamb for hours, calling out to each other as they searched. "Te dît? Te dît?" (teh deet teh deet), which means in Kurdish "You see it? You see it?"

"Ne dît" (neh deet), Ne dît."

Owl (Kund).

"I don't. I don't," was always the reply.

They never returned. In fact, in time they turned into owls. They are always out in the night calling to each other and searching for their lost little lamb.

Note: Collected in October 2005 from Çeto Ozel, Colemêrg (Hakkari) region, Kurmancî and English.

Why the Magpie Has a Long Tail

*T*hey say this: they say that the magpie was once human like us. In long-ago times, the magpie was not a bird but a peddler who traveled from village to village carrying on his back the things he had to sell. In those days, there were no markets in the village, so the people relied on peddlers to bring them the goods that they couldn't make themselves.

This peddler always cheated his customers. One of his special tricks was to measure out less cloth than the people paid for. If they paid for one meter, he would only give them eighty or ninety centimeters. He never gave them an honest amount.

The peddler was always on the road before the people discovered that he had swindled them. And, though they tried, no one was ever able to catch him. But at last Xwedê (kweh-day) punished him. He changed that peddler into a magpie and attached to his back forever his long measuring stick. That was to remind him that he should have taken care of the people, measuring out for them exactly what they paid for.

Magpie (Keşkele/Qirik).

Note: Collected in May 2005 from a fifty-five-year-old woman, Bitlîs region, Kurmancî.

Bear and Hair: Hirch û Pirch

Women prepare sheep's wool for bedding and to spin into yarn, 2006. Photo by the author.

Yek hebû û yek tûnebû . . .[1] Once there was and once there wasn't a rich man who had a large flock of sheep. It was the middle of May, the time when the sheep must be sheared because if their heavy wool is left on, they suffer from the heat. The rich man was standing near his shepherd watching him as he cut the wool from the sheep. In the distance, he saw an old man coming toward them down the road. The old man was leaning on a walking stick and his clothes were just rags. His beard was very long. You could tell just by looking at him that he was very poor and didn't have anyone at all to help him or take care of him.

Now the wealthy man knew that if any poor person came, he would be expected to give them some wool. The winters in Kurdistan are very cold, and those who don't have any animals need wool for their sweaters, hats, gloves, and socks and to make blankets to keep out the cold. But what the wealthy man didn't know was that this old man was really Xizir (khih-zihr) in disguise.[2] For the Alevi (ah-leh-vee) Kurds, Xizir is a very holy figure. If they are in need, they call on him, and he will always be there to help them. The Alevis also know that at any time Xizir may come in some disguise to test them to see if they are doing good or not.

This wealthy man had a selfish spirit and didn't want to give away any of his wool. He said to his shepherd, "If that old man asks you for wool, tell him that the owner isn't here and that's why you can't give him any." Then he buried himself in his big pile of wool. He covered himself from top to bottom with it and pretended he wasn't there.

Disguised as a poor old man, Xizir approached and asked, "Could you please give me the wool from one of your animals?" "I can't give you anything," said the shepherd, "because the owner isn't here."

But Xizir knew everything. He knew the owner was hiding underneath the wool. Xizir took his walking stick and brought it down on the rich man hiding in the wool. Three times he hit him with the stick.

"Hirch û pirch!" (hihrch oo pihrch)

"Hirch û pirch!"

"Hirch û pirch!"

"Bear and hair!"—that is what he said three times.

"Since you cover yourself in this wool and do not wish to part from it, from now on animal hair will cling to you and cover you from head to toe. Your face shall evermore be turned to the wilderness. You will never again know the comfort of your own home."

It came to pass as Xizir said. The wool clung to the man and became as thick as fur. He turned into a bear and went up into the mountains. He lost everything and became like an animal. Sometimes bears can seem very human, but they always go towards the wilderness.

The lesson of this story is that we should share whatever we have with others. The story tells us not to be very hungry and keep everything for ourselves. If you don't share, you become like an animal. You become very selfish. When people are selfish, they can kill each other. They always want to be richer and more powerful. This story says we shouldn't strive for that. It tells us to share. When you share, you become beautiful.

Notes: This tale is based on versions collected in 2006–2007 from Gulcem Aktas, Gimgim (Varto) region, Dimilî, and English, and from Saadat Fidan and Elmas Fidan, Sivas region, village of Kello, Kurmancî. (The version told by the Fidans was collected and translated with the help of Yuksel Serindag.)

1. Yek hebû û yek tûnebû . . . (yehk heh-boo oo yehk too-neh-boo) is one of the traditional beginnings of a Kurdish tale. It means "once there was and once there wasn't."

2. Xizir is a divine and godlike figure among the Alevis (a Kurdish religious group). Xizir is believed to protect and to guide them. In times of need, he is called on for help, and he is always nearby. In the month of February, the Alevis fast for three days in honor of Xizir. Afterwards, bicik (bih-jihk) a large, round bread, is baked and shared with neighbors (see bicik on page 12). A Xizir evening is held at a designated holy family's house. This holy family prepares a meal for all the guests and then the rêyber or pîr (a religious guide or hereditary leader of the group) begins to sing divine music upon the saz (sahz), a stringed instrument. He calls upon God and Xizir. At that time, people often participate in Sema (seh-mah) dances, which are semihypnotic and rhythmic ritual dances.

Bear (Hirch/Wirch).

Bear and Hair: Hirch û Pirch

Fox Tales!

Bila dijminê meriv şêr be, ne rovî be!

May your enemy be a lion, not a fox!

—**Kurdish Proverb**

The Kurdish people have many stories in which the animals speak and act like humans. Especially enjoyed are stories about Rovî (Fox) and his attempts to outwit those around him. Everyone laughs when they hear about his adventures. "Oh, Fox is so cunning!" the audience will say as Fox triumphs in yet another difficult situation. But it is just as enjoyable when a weaker animal at last takes its revenge on "Uncle" Fox.

Fox and Stork

*I*n the high mountains where foxes live, a fox set out to amuse himself one day. In his travels, he came across a stork. They introduced themselves and then set off together, strolling around until it was evening.

While they were walking, the fox thought of all the terrible things he could do to the stork. He wanted to continue to spend time with her and amuse himself by playing some tricks. When they were about to part, the fox said, "Madame Stork, I'm very happy I met you. I'd like to invite you to be my guest tomorrow morning, so that we can share a meal together."

"Oh, Uncle Fox," the stork replied, "I'm not used to going places just on invitation alone. However, I don't want to break a dear friend's heart like yours, so tomorrow I will come and be your guest."

"Oh then, I'll be waiting early for you! The earlier you come the better!" said the fox.

In the morning, just before the stork arrived, Uncle Fox cooked up some lentil soup. When he saw his guest approaching, he poured the soup out, all over a great flat board. Uncle Fox graciously brought Madame Stork over to the board where the soup was spread all over.

Stork (Legleg).

"To tell you the truth, this kind of meal isn't good enough for such a beautiful guest as you," he said, "but what can I do? This is all I have to prepare for you, so let's start eating."

The stork pecked and pecked at the soup, but she could barely pick anything up. It was so dry and it bothered the stork so much that her heart ached. When the fox saw that the stork couldn't possibly eat the soup, he laughed to himself. He didn't say a word, but enjoyed licking up every last bit of soup from the board, chuckling all the while.

When he was finished, he was quite full and said, "I hope you enjoyed this breakfast. Although we are only foxes, we try to show as much respect as we can to our guests. If I do have any shortcomings, I hope you'll forgive me."

After this strange breakfast, the hungry stork began to realize that the cunning fox was making fun of her. However, she didn't say anything about this. She just behaved as if she were full. She thanked the fox and said, "Because you showed me respect and you behaved so well to me, I would also like you to be my guest. If you come, we will have a meal and we will have a talk about the worries and the problems of the world." The stork looked so sincere that the fox didn't understand that she was planning her revenge. He accepted the invitation.

In the morning before the fox came, the stork cooked up some chickpeas and, just as he had done, she poured the breakfast out. But she poured her chickpeas into a deep hole in the ground. This hole had such a narrow opening that the fox's mouth could never fit in to reach the food.

When the stork saw that the fox was coming, she went out to meet him and brought him directly to the tiny hole. The fox walked around the hole. He tried to reach the food with his tongue. The first time he tried he managed to eat a few chickpeas, but then he couldn't reach anymore. The stork with its narrow beak ate and ate and got very full. When the chickpeas were all gone, Uncle Fox said, "Madame Stork, I am well aware that you've had your revenge on me. In this matter it's obvious that you're much more cunning than I, and you're much more successful. There is a saying—and it's not said for nothing—that 'two powerful rulers cannot live in the same place.' Those two rulers are you and I."

The stork pretended she didn't understand what the fox was talking about. Still the fox continued to lecture her about serving him chickpeas in that narrow hole. When the fox finally finished speaking, the stork acted as though she were hurt and offended. She said to him, "Believe me, I didn't do that on purpose. I even thought that a meal of chickpeas would be something new for you and that you would like it. You can see that I tried my best. Who would think that your mouth couldn't reach the chickpeas in that hole. I have never been so sorry, and I hope that you'll forgive me for this failing."

Uncle Fox looked at the stork's face, which was filled with sadness and regret, and he believed that she hadn't done it on purpose.

"Don't worry about it, nobody's perfect," he told her. "These things can happen even without our willing them. Sometimes, even without knowing it, brothers kill each other. Don't think about it anymore, what happened, happened. The past is past."

"How can you say that?" Madame Stork replied. I can't stop thinking about how I didn't know that hole was too narrow. No matter what, I will make this up to you. As you know, not everyone has the gift to fly that I have. If you want, I'll take you up into the air so you can look around and have some fun."

The fox was very happy about this idea. He accepted Madame Stork's invitation, but then he hesitated and said doubtfully, "Everyone knows that I go a lot of places and that traveling is something wonderful for me. But up until now I've never been up in the sky. Do you think I'll be safe there?"

"Uncle Fox, don't be scared. Just hang onto my wings and nothing will happen."

When she said this, the fox was happy. The stork opened up her wings. Without any hesitation, the fox climbed on and the stork flew up into the sky. Higher and higher she flew.

"Madame Stork," said the fox, "I'm getting scared. If you fly a bit lower maybe I won't be so afraid."

The stork didn't listen to him and continued to fly even higher.

"How does the ground look to you now, Uncle Fox?"

"It looks wonderful! I can even see some chickens around the houses in the village."

"How greedy you are that all you can think about are chickens. You shouldn't be thinking about chickens—you're up in the air having a wonderful trip. Why are you still thinking about them?"

"What can I do?" said Uncle Fox happily. "I like them! I love them! I love them so much that wherever I am I look for them."

"Now look down. How does the ground look to you now?"

"It seems as if there's a white mist on the ground. If you ask me, please don't go any higher. It will be much better if we descend now."

"All right, if that's what you would like. But now my wings are frozen. Hold on because I'll have to pull them in to dive down."

Suddenly the stork veered off to the side. She leaned and leaned until Uncle Fox fell off and tumbled to the ground. In this way Madame Stork got her revenge for being served lentil soup on a board.

Uncle Fox fell down and met his end . . . and Madame Stork? She flew away and took the rest of our story with her.

Note: Collected by Abbas Alkan and published in his book *Çîroka Rovî û Gur* [*Tales of Fox and Wolf*], published in 2003 by Weşanên Elma, Istanbul, Turkey, Kurmancî. Translated by Çeto Ozel.

And Fox Will Have His Tail Back

The Kurdish word for "old woman" is "pîrê" (peer-ay). A pîrê will often appear in the stories. It is no wonder, as elderly Kurdish women—strong, wise and resilient—are quite a force to be reckoned with. They are very important not only for the stories but for the culture. In this story, I have substituted the Kurdish word "pîrê" for "old woman." It fits in the best with the great rhythm of this tale.

Elderly woman, 2006. Photo by the author.

*O*nce there was a pîrê. Every day she brought her milk home, and every night a fox snuck in and drank it. One night, two nights, three nights, four, she hid herself to see who was drinking the milk. Along came a fox. The pîrê took a heavy scythe, and as the fox was going past her, she cut off his tail.

The fox ran back to his friends, and when they saw him, they teased him saying, "You had a close shave! Just look at you! Bobtail! Bobtail! Wherever you came from, go back there! You are really funny-looking!" His friends didn't like him now at all.

The fox went back to the pîrê and said to her, "All my friends are making fun of me. Please give me my tail back." The pîrê said, "Bring me my milk and I will give you your tail back!"

Fox went to the goat and said, "Goat, Goat, give me milk. If you give me milk, Pîrê will give me my tail back." The goat said, "Bring me grass and I will give you milk so that Pîrê will give you your tail back."

Fox went to the grass and said, "Grass, Grass, give me grass. If you give me grass I can feed the goat, who'll give me milk so that Pîrê will give me my tail back." The grass said, "Bring me a scythe and I'll give you grass, to feed the goat, who'll give you milk so that Pîrê will give you your tail back."

So Fox went to the blacksmith and said "Blacksmith, Blacksmith, make me a scythe. If you make me a scythe I can cut the grass, to feed the goat, who'll give me milk so that Pîrê will give me my tail back." The blacksmith said, "Bring me eggs and I'll make you a scythe, to cut the grass, to feed the goat, who'll give you milk so that Pîrê will give you your tail back."

Fox went to the hen and said, "Hen, Hen, give me eggs. If you give me eggs, I can feed the blacksmith, who'll make a scythe, to cut the grass, to feed the goat, who'll give me milk so that Pîrê will give me my tail back." The hen said, "Bring me wheat and I'll give you eggs, to feed the blacksmith, who'll make a scythe, to cut the grass, to feed the goat, who'll give you milk so that Pîrê will give you your tail back."

Fox went to a granary where there was a pile of wheat and he said, "Wheat, Wheat, give me wheat. If you give me wheat I can feed the hen, who'll lay the eggs, to feed the blacksmith, who'll make a scythe, to cut the grass, to feed the goat, who'll give me milk so that Pîrê will give me my tail back." The pile of wheat said "It's a little drafty in here and the rain comes in through that hole in the wall. Fix the hole with some mud and I'll give you wheat, to feed the hen, who'll lay the eggs, to feed the blacksmith, who'll make a scythe, to cut the grass, to feed the goat, who'll give you milk so that Pîrê will give you your tail back."

Fox fixed the hole. Wheat gave wheat, hen laid eggs, eggs fed blacksmith, blacksmith made scythe, scythe cut grass, grass fed goat, goat gave milk, Fox gave the milk to Pîrê and Pîrê gave Fox his tail back.

BUT . . . before she gave Fox his tail back, she tied lots of cans and mirrors, bells, and ringers all over it. So when he went back to his friends this time, he was making a lot of pretty noise.

His friends said, "Wow, where did you get all of those beautiful decorations on your tail?" Fox said "Don't you know that if you stick your tail in the freezing cold river and leave it there overnight you get all these nice bells and mirrors on your tail, just like I have?" "Great!" said his friends and they stuck their tails into the freezing river and kept them there all night long. The next morning the ice had frozen, and when they tried to pull their tails out, they pulled them right off. Then our fox laughed and laughed at them saying, "Bobtail! Bobtail! You are really funny-looking!"

Now my story is told, and whoever is listening to me, God grant their mothers and their fathers compassion.

Note: From several versions collected in 2002–2006, Kurmancî and Dimilî.

A Fox Is Not a Lion

ek hebû û yek tûnebû . . . Once there was and once there wasn't a lion. He was relaxing in the shade of some trees, when a fox passed by.

"Hey Fox!" the lion called out. "What are you looking for around here?"

The fox said, "Great master, with respect, I'm looking for something to eat. I'm very hungry, so hungry that I can't even see my way."

The lion felt sorry for the fox and said to him, "If you give up your cunning ways, I will give you a place to live and feed you the hindquarters of sheep for your dinner."

Well, of course, foxes love to eat just that part of the sheep. It's their favorite food if they can get it. The fox said, "If you would do such a thing for me, I would be your servant and I would never disobey you." The lion stood up and said, "Follow me."

The fox and the lion walked together until they came across a flock of sheep. They stopped there. The lion told the fox, "I'll run around to warm up. When my eyes get red, tell me, because that means I'm ready." The fox said, "OK, my master, I understand." The lion ran up and down the mountain until his eyes were red.

"Master, your eyes are as red as two glowing embers," said the fox.

The lion stopped, looked at the flock of sheep, and leapt into the flock, capturing one of the sheep. The shepherd and the dogs guarding the flock couldn't do anything because they were too afraid. The lion killed the sheep right there and brought it over to the fox. Together they went to the lion's den. The lion gave the hindquarters of the sheep to the fox and ate the rest himself.

The fox stayed with the lion a long time. The fox got fed, and he had a nice life and good days. He had forgotten all about his old life and his hunger, but his heart was still full of deceit and disloyal thoughts. He said to himself, "Why should I be the servant of this lion? I can do whatever he does. I should find a way to get rid of him so that I can be the ruler of this place." The fox spent the day thinking of all the tricky things he could do to the lion.

One day, as the lion and the fox were talking to each other in the den, the fox said, "Master Lion, if you would permit me, I wish to ask you a question."

"What is your question?" asked the lion.

"Master Lion, today a mouse said to me, 'Do you know how to tie up a lion so that it can't escape?' I said, 'No, I don't,' and the mouse laughed at me saying, 'I know this and you don't, and you say that you are the lion's servant! Ha! Ha! Ha!' Master Lion, I was very embarrassed when the mouse made fun of me like that. Will you please tell me how you can be tied?"

The lion was taken in by the story the fox told and he replied, "A lion can be tied by its own hair."

"How?" asked the fox.

"If someone takes the hair from our tail and ties our paws together with it, then we cannot escape no matter how hard we try. But don't tell these things to anybody."

"Master Lion, do you think I'm crazy? Why would I say these things to anybody else?"

One dark night, the fox woke up. He couldn't fall back to sleep because he couldn't stop thinking all his terrible thoughts about betraying the lion. Finally, he got up and crept over to the lion. He could see that he was fast asleep. Cautiously and anxiously the fox severed three long hairs from the lion's tail. Then he quickly tied the lion's paws together and got out of the den. He left the lion as he was, and ran away.

At dawn, the fox was strolling around the mountain. After a while he saw two other foxes and said to them.

"Listen you two, become my servants and I'll feed you on the hindquarters of sheep every day."

"How can you do that?" one of the foxes asked.

"If you accept and become my servants, I'll show you."

The two foxes accepted, and they all went along together until they came near a flock of sheep.

"I'm going to run up and down the mountain to warm up. When my eyes become red, you tell me, because that means I'm ready," said the fox.

The fox ran up and down and up and down.

"Are my eyes red?" he asked his friends.

"No," they said.

The fox went on running up and down. Always he asked if his eyes were red, and always his friends said no. His friends knew that his eyes would never get red, and they said to each other, "He'll get exhausted from all this. Let's just tell him that his eyes are red and see what he'll do." The fox again ran down from the mountain and asked his friends if his eyes were red. This time his friends told him, "Yes, your eyes are very red now."

Our fox jumped into the flock of sheep and tried to catch one. The sheep were scared and started to run and the shepherd stood up and saw that there was a fox in the flock. "Catch him! Catch him!" the shepherd shouted to his dogs. The dogs caught the fox right away. The shepherd came, and with his shepherd's crook he beat the fox. Because of the shepherd's beating and the dog's biting, the fox shouted until he died, "Now I know for sure—a fox is not a lion!"

And what about our lion? He was still tied up in his den, so exhausted from hunger and anger that he couldn't do anything.

One day, a mouse came out of its hole and saw the lion. At first, the mouse was afraid, but when it saw that the lion was tied up, it wasn't afraid anymore. The mouse felt sorry for the lion and with its teeth it gnawed through the hair that tied the lion's paws. The lion jumped to its feet and ran away saying, "A place where a fox can tie up a lion and a mouse can set him free will never be my home!" And he left that place forever.

Note: Collected in October 2005 from Çeto Ozel, Colmêrg (Hakkari) region, Kurmancî and English.

Fox Goes on a Pilgrimage

There are several references to Islamic religious practices in this Fox tale. Fox mentions that the duck is "always washing," preparing itself for prayer, referring to the custom of devotees to wash both hands and feet before praying. And Fox appeals to the vanity of the birds by calling them "Imams" meaning Islamic religious leaders or scholars. In the story, Fox invites the birds to go on a pilgrimage, to Mecca. In the Muslim religion, this is one of the most important events that can happen in a person's life. The one who has gone on a pilgrimage and returned is called a hacî (hah-jee), a pilgrim. New pilgrims sometimes wear a shawl-like covering, signifying that they have been to the holy land. There are many stories about wily Fox dressing up as a devout pilgrim and taking some birds with him on a religious journey. This is one of my favorites.

One day a fox went down to the water's edge where a duck was quacking and swimming about in the water.

"*Quh-toh, quh-toh, quh-toh, quh-toh, quh-toh,*" went the duck.

"Oh the beautiful duck!" said the fox. "Oh, the Imam with the green head! You are always washing yourself for prayer, but why do you splash about in these waters? Come where you will be appreciated. Let's be friends and go on a pilgrimage together. Look, I am Hacî Mohammed (Mohammed's pilgrim). I have covered my head with a scarf."

The duck flew over to the other side of the lake.

"I don't trust you," said the duck, "I never trust your cunning ways."

"Oh," said the fox meekly. "I promise I will never attack you or even touch you. I am Hacî Mohammed. Come with me and we will eat the hen of the pilgrim together."[1]

"*Quh-toh, quh-toh, quh-toh, quh-toh, quh-toh!* All right!" said the duck and it started waddling along beside him.

They came to a village where a rooster was crowing from the top of a stable announcing it was morning. "*Keeeeeeeeeee keh deeeeee,*" said the rooster.

"Oh herald of the Imam's," called out the fox, "why are you announcing the morning call to prayer here? Come with us on a pilgrimage to the holy places where the beauty of your singing will be much more appreciated. Let's be friends and travel all together. You see I have covered my head with a scarf. We will eat the hen of the pilgrim together."

"But you are my greatest enemy in the world," the rooster replied. "How can I be your friend?"

"The duck became my friend," said the fox, "and now we are going on a pilgrimage together."

"I will never accept that," said the rooster.

The duck waddled over to the rooster saying, "*Quh-toh, quh-toh, quh-toh, quh-toh, quh-toh.*"

"*Keeeeeeeeeee keh deeeeee,*" crowed the rooster.

After that interesting conversation, the rooster changed its mind. It fell in line with the duck and the fox, and they all went down the road together.

Later that morning, they came across a partridge standing on a rock.

"*Kah-kuh Woh, Kah-kuh Woh, Kah-kuh Woh, Kah-kuh Woh, Kah! Kah! Kah! Kah!*" said the partridge.

"Oh, beautiful Imam!" said the fox. "Why are you praying on this rock? You deserve to be standing at the Mosque of the Prophet.[2] Come on a pilgrimage with me and we will eat the hen of the pilgrim together."

"You are my enemy," said the partridge, "How can you say that we should be friends? You will kill me!"

"In the name of God, I promise you I will not. Look, I have covered my head with a scarf," said the fox. "Be my friend and we will all go on a pilgrimage together."

"*Kah-kuh Woh, Kah-kuh Woh, Kah-kuh Woh, Kah-kuh Woh!* All right!" said the partridge. And the partridge joined them.

Down the road they went, but as time passed, the fox began to get hungry. He whispered to the duck, "You were the first one that I asked to go on a pilgrimage with me, so I won't eat you. I'll eat this rooster." "If you eat him, you'll eat me too," said the duck. And the fox went after the rooster.

"I knew you were not to be trusted," said the partridge and it flew a safe distance away.

The fox made a meal out of the rooster. He ate the head, and then he finished off everything else. The duck and the partridge talked amongst themselves.

"*Quh-toh, quh-toh, quh-toh, quh-toh, quh-toh!*"

"*Kah-kuh Woh, Kah-kuh Woh, Kah-kuh Woh, Kah-kuh Woh!*"

"Why did the fox do that?" asked the partridge. "Didn't we promise each other to be friends?"

"But the fox was very hungry," said the duck. "Well, what's done is done. Let's continue on the pilgrimage together, just us three."

They only traveled a short way when the fox attacked and ate the partridge. Now only the duck was left, but God gave the duck the gift of flight, and it flew to the middle of a lake.

The fox ran around and around the lake calling out to the duck. "Come closer, come closer and pray!"

"No!" said the duck, "You told me we would go on a pilgrimage and eat the hen of the hacî and instead you ate the partridge and you ate the rooster and now you're going to eat me."

"I promise you on my honor I will not," the fox replied. "I am Hacî Mohammed. Come with me. We only have one day left to travel. The rooster and the partridge are gone, so it's no use thinking about them, but you and I can go on together. Come!"

The duck came nearer and the fox swam out a little, and then the fox opened up his mouth and ate up the duck too.

Now our story has flown out to the land,
And there our ancestors will catch it in their hand.

Notes: Collected in June 2006 from a thirty-eight-year-old man, Mukus region, Kurmancî.

1. It is not quite clear what is being referred to here. The fox might be saying that the food eaten by a pilgrim would be special food or he might be making a clever reference to what his favorite food might be.

2. The Mosque of the Prophet, in Medina, Saudi Arabia, is considered one of Islam's most important religious sites. It is the final resting place of Mohammed, the founder of Islam.

Fox, The Basket Maker!

Yek hebû û yek tûnebû... Once there was and once there wasn't an old fox. He was looking for a new place to live because his old home had been overrun with wolves and other dangerous creatures. The fox passed through many mountains, valleys, and forests, looking for a place that would be suitable. After traveling high up into the mountains, he found a nice spot and settled in. To get to know it well he explored all around looking for things to eat. What else could a poor fox do? He wasn't a snake to feed himself with the soil.[1]

**Kurdish carrying basket, 2006.
Photo by the author.**

Sometimes he would make his way into a village, catch a chicken, and eat it. After a while the hunters realized this, and they put traps everywhere for the old fox. They even put traps on the path he always used. But the fox was experienced. He knew they were after him, and he always found a clever way to avoid their traps.

One day the fox heard that, without his knowing it, a wolf had snuck into his territory. The fox was very angry because of this and thought to himself, "The best thing to do would be to trick the wolf into going over the traps that are set for me. Then he'll be killed, and I'll be rid of him." After he had come up with these clever thoughts, he went out looking for the wolf. He searched for several days before he saw the wolf heading in his direction. The old fox called out with sweet and friendly words. "Hey Brother, I heard there was a wolf in the area, and I was just thinking about you! They say that when you mention a good person's name they appear, and here you are![2] You have come to the right place. For a long time I have been looking for a friend like you. You're welcome to come along with me. I think you may be hungry, are you?"

When the wolf saw how friendly the fox was, he thought he could take advantage of him. He planned on learning all that the fox knew and then killing him or forcing him out so that he would be the owner of the region. Lots and lots of nasty things went through the wolf's mind, but he only said, "Brother Fox, thank you. I don't know the area and I'm hungry and exhausted from walking around and searching for food." The wolf spoke sweetly and used the same deceitful methods as the fox!

"So, let's have something to eat and then relax." said the fox. "Come, I'll show you every inch of this place."

The fox and the wolf spent the day exploring and at last the fox brought the wolf over to the path where the hunters had set their traps. They walked for a while down the path and then the fox said, "Brother Wolf, you go on ahead of me. I need to relieve myself, but travel slowly and I will catch up with you." The wolf had been planning on getting rid of the fox all along, and happily walked away. In just a few moments though, his two front paws were caught in one of the traps. He howled in pain. When the old fox heard the cries of the wolf, he came to take a peek. He laughed to himself when he saw the wolf struggling to be free and then slunk off into the forest. The wolf, however, did not give up. He pulled and twisted and, with difficulty, got out of the trap. He was furious and immediately started following the trail of the fox so that he could get his revenge.

The cunning old fox was happily strolling in the forest when he saw the wolf heading his way. He immediately collected a lot of sticks and started busily making baskets. When the wolf arrived, the fox was sitting peacefully, making baskets as if he hadn't seen the wolf approaching at all.

The wolf limped over to the fox and said angrily, "You lousy, good for nothing! You idiot! You took me down a bad road and if I hadn't rescued myself, the hunters would have killed me in the morning." The old fox looked surprised. "Uncle Wolf, what on earth are you talking about? Are you crazy or just confused? This place is full of foxes. I swear I'm not the fox who did these things to you. It should be obvious that I'm not the one you're after because I have sworn never to do bad things to anyone. It's been years and years since I did anything naughty. You can see I'm earning my living by making and selling baskets. I buy bread to eat with the money I earn."

After hearing the fox's words, the wolf began to calm down. He really believed that the old fox was a basket maker. He still needed someone to show him around the territory, so he pretended to befriend the fox.

"Forgive me, Brother Fox, for saying those things to you considering that you have sworn never to do any harm to anyone. I also swear never to do anything wrong. And, if you like, I will work with you and make baskets and earn my living just like you do."

The fox knew the wolf's intentions and laughed to himself. He accepted the friendship of the wolf and then continued weaving baskets as though no one was there. The wolf walked around the fox and became impatient.

"Brother Wolf," said the fox, "you are my guest, and I don't want to make you work, but, if you want to learn how to make baskets, just come and sit in the middle of this basket so that it won't shake. In that way you can see how I'm making it and you will learn."

Just as the old fox requested, the wolf got into the half-finished basket and sat down. The fox thought to himself, "This time, I'll fool him so that I will never again come across him or have to speak with him. I'll save myself and I won't ever be in danger from him again."

The fox slowly went on making the basket. He wove slower and slower and slower and the wolf fell asleep in the basket. The moment the fox saw this he quickly tied all the loose ends of the basket together until there was no way for the wolf to escape. He tipped the basket on its side and rolled it toward the village. With the rolling motion, the wolf woke up. He yelled and howled.

When the dogs of the village saw the basket rolling down the hill toward them, and heard a wolf's voice coming from it, they attacked. They dragged the wolf out of the basket and played with him. He saved himself from the dogs with great difficulty.

As soon as he got rid of the dogs, the wolf went chasing after the fox. When the fox saw that the wolf was after him again, he said to himself, "This wolf is going to force me to kill him!"

The fox deliberately ran so that the wolf would follow him. He made him exhausted by running him up and down the mountains. At last he brought the wolf near to where he had his den. The den's entryway was just big enough for a fox. The fox slowed down until the wolf was right on his tail and then suddenly dove into his den. The wolf was right behind him and got stuck in the hole.

The fox was full of pluck.
He saw the wolf was stuck.
He walked around Wolf's head
And this is what he said,
"So, Wolf you've traveled very far
But in my den is where you are.
You thought to feast on fox's food
You were so cunning and so rude.
The war you started was a sin
A war with fox is hard to win.
We fight up high on mountaintop.
We fight down low, we never stop.
We lead you up, we lead you down
And now I'll leave you in the ground."

The old fox killed the wolf and left our story there.

Notes: Collected by Abbas Alkan and published in his book *Çîroka Rovî û Gur* [*Tales of Fox and Wolf*], published in 2003 by Weşanên Elma, Istanbul, Turkey, Kurmancî. Translated by Çeto Ozel.

1. There is a saying in Kurdistan, "Ma ez mar im bi axê bijim," which means, "Am I a snake to live by earth alone?" It was believed at one time that snakes could live by eating soil. This saying is presently used when someone is out of work and has almost nothing to live on.

2. There is an old saying in Kurdistan that if the person you speak of is good, then very soon you will see them.

Kurdistan is a land of contrasts with steep mountains, green valleys, and rushing streams, 2006. Photo by the author.

Clothes are set out to dry in the fresh air, 2006. Photo by the author.

Winding roads lead to a Kurdish village nestled among trees and surrounded by steep mountains, 2006. Photo by the author.

Govend, or line dances, are an
important part of life in Kurdistan.
Each region has its own unique
dances. Dances can be for men
only, women only, or for both men
and women. Photos courtesy of
Çeto Ozel.

As the snow melts, it creates
a mottled green and white
pattern called belekevî.
Underneath the snow the
rich underlying zozan
(highland plain) is revealed,
2006. Photo by the author.

Sheep gather on the snow in early May to take advantage of the salt that has been put out there for them, 2006. Photo by the author.

The animals are brought to the same bêrî (place for milking) daily. Here several bêrîvan (milkmaids) gather to milk the goats, 2006. Photo by the author.

After the goats and sheep have been milked, those who have helped journey home together, 2006. Photo by the author.

Fertile banks line the winding rivers of Kurdistan where both high mountains and pastoral landscapes abound, 2005. Photo courtesy of Tom Megan.

A young boy uses a stick to lead two oxen as they plow a steep hillside. Behind the cotkar (ploughman) comes the farmer scattering the seed, 2006. Photo by the author.

Gold jewelry shines from the store windows of shops in Wan (Van). Gold is important at weddings, where it is worn by the bride or given as a gift, 2006. Photo by the author.

A couple pauses for their picture to be taken, circa 1955. Photo courtesy of Rudman Ham.

A woman spins using a teshî (spindle). Her young child stands beside her, circa 1955. Photo courtesy of Rudman Ham.

The teashop is a favorite gathering place for men to talk, drink tea (çay) and share stories, 2006. Photo by the author.

Two women stand on the rooftops of Shaqlawa, a mountainous town near Hewlêr (Erbil), spinning wool into thread, circa 1955. Photo courtesy of Rudman Ham.

A woman removes bread that has been baking in the tandoor (a deep clay oven or metal-lined fire pit), 2006. Photo by the author.

Kurdish men work side by side as they harvest wheat, circa 1955. Photo courtesy of Rudman Ham.

A young girl and her brother watch over the sheep for their family, 2006. Photo by the author.

First encounter between a young boy and a colt, 2006. Photo by the author.

People spend time outdoors upon their rooftops in this early picture of Shaqlawa, in Iraqi Kurdistan. In the upper left corner of the picture, people gather at a church for an upcoming wedding, circa 1955. Photo courtesy of Rudman Ham.

Television has come to the remote mountain villages. It is a common sight to see satellite dishes on even the oldest houses, 2006. Photo by the author.

Separated from family members or grazing grounds by what they see as artificially drawn boundaries, Kurds often cross the borders of the nation-states that divide them. In this photo, Kurdish nomads travel from Iranian Kurdistan to Iraqi Kurdistan. The women wear traditional headdresses, circa 1955. Photo courtesy of Rudman Ham.

A woman on horseback pauses on her way to the bêrî, the place where the sheep and goats are milked, 2006. Photo by the author.

Tales of Wonder

Hoste necar razê weke her car, Xwedê yek e dergeh hezar.

Master craftsman rest easy, there is one God but
one thousand doorways.

—Kurdish Proverb

Shaqlawa wedding: the bride, seated on the horse in the right-hand side of the picture, is arriving at the groom's house. Iraqi Kurdistan, circa 1955. Photo courtesy of Rudman Ham.

The Eggs of the Ancient Tree

In this story, reference is made to the berbûk (behr-book), the bridal party that is responsible for escorting the bride to the groom's house for the wedding. The berbûk consists of female relatives of the groom and other young girls from the village. Colorfully dressed and covered with a shawl, the bride is placed upon a horse for the journey. The bride's relatives cry as she is leaving, for now she will become part of the groom's family forever. The berbûk assists the bride all along the way and accompanies her journey with singing and dancing. Traditional instruments for these processions include the davul and the zurna. The davul is an ancient type of frame drum. One side is covered in thick sheepskin and played with a heavy stick. The other side is covered in thin goatskin and played with a light stick to produce a much higher tone. The zurna is a double reed instrument with a two-octave range, similar in sound to an oboe. The groom stands on the roof of his home and when the bride comes into the yard, he showers her with candies. In earlier times, walnuts and raisins would be used. If the groom's family is rich, he showers her with money. The groom tosses an apple at his bride as a token that he will take her to be his "apple love." All of the families from the village or region gather for the wedding. The celebration, which is like a festival, may go on for three days or for several weeks depending on the status of the family.

*Y*ek hebû û yek tûnebû . . . Once there was and once there wasn't an old woman. As she was on her way to a nearby stream to fill her jug with water, the son of the Padishah blocked her way with his horse. He didn't let her pass because he wanted his horse to drink first. Twice she tried to fill her jug and twice he spun his horse around to stop her. The old woman cursed him saying, "Because of how you have treated me, an old woman, my curse is that you must now go in search of the eggs of the ancient tree."

The young man rode his horse back home and told his parents everything that had happened. "Son, don't try to do this," said his father, the Padishah. "It will be a long and dangerous way. Who knows where this tree may be." Both of his parents tried to dissuade him, but they couldn't stop him. So they put a lot of gold and other things he might need for the journey into his saddlebag and he rode away.

He traveled far and he traveled long. At last he came upon a Sufi sitting by the side of the road. This mystical holy man was patiently knitting a large sack; his beard was long and white. "Son, where are you going?" asked the Sufi. The youth told him his story and the Sufi

replied, "Don't go on this journey. There are foxes and bears lying in wait all along the way and they will devour you."

"Even so," said the youth, "I will go. If you have good advice, please give it to me now. Otherwise, I will be on my way."

"Is your decision made? Are you really going?"

"Yes," said the youth.

"Well then, I do have some advice. You will have to travel far and it will take a long time, but at last you will come to a plateau high up in the mountains. There you'll find a hidden field. There will be muddy places and there will be water. But you will know you have found the right place because it will be so fertile and green, everywhere green. Only one tree grows on this plain. This is the ancient tree full of eggs. Dig a well nearby that will be big enough for you to hide in. You will have to dig deeply. Take care that it will hide you completely. Once your hiding place is certain, go to the tree and take one egg. As soon as you take the egg, hide yourself because the tree will ring, and many dangerous animals from all over the world will come. If they see you, they will eat you. Do the same thing a second and a third time until you have three eggs."

"Thank you very much for your advice," said the son of the Padishah. He gave the old man some gold and went on his way.

He traveled and traveled, on and on, until he found that fertile field with one lone tree in the middle of it. He knew he had found the place that the Sufi spoke of, and he was very happy at this. The first thing he did was to dig a deep well. "All right," he said to himself, "I will pick one egg and then hide myself. Let's see what's going to happen."

When he picked an egg from the tree, all of the eggs on the tree began to vibrate and ring out. "Ching, ching, ching," was the sound they made. He quickly jumped into the well he had dug and listened to what was going on outside. Bears, wolves, and other wild animals gathered around the tree. They searched and looked everywhere, but they couldn't find anyone near the tree or even up the tree. The youth waited until they had gone. He went a second time to the tree, taking an egg and then hiding in the well. Again the tree rang and the wild animals came. They looked everywhere, but they couldn't find the youth. He stayed hidden a long time until they were finally gone. He said to himself, "This third time is my last task, and I have to do it." When he took the third egg, the eggs on the tree vibrated and rang loudly. But this time he didn't hide; he saved himself by galloping away on his horse.

He rode and rode as far as he could. At last, tired and hungry, he got down from his horse and sat down to rest in the shade of a tree by the river. "Xwedê zane" (kweh-day zah-nah), "God knows," he said to himself. "We will see what God knows and what God will create."

He prepared a simple lunch for himself of bread and water. "I will break one of the eggs," he thought. "I hope that when I break it, I won't regret it." When he broke the egg it spoke saying, "Bread and water, bread and water," and then it disappeared. He broke the second egg and it also said, "Bread and water, bread and water" and then disappeared. "I have only one egg left," he said. "Xwedê, please help me and don't make me regret this." He broke the third egg and it said, "Bread and water, bread and water," but this egg did not disappear, it turned into a beautiful perî (peh-ree), a fairy from heaven. The son of the Padishah was so happy. His heart softened, and he thought, "She is so beautiful. The only thing I want is to marry her." Now he had truly achieved his aim, but he was torn as to what to do next. He knew it would be improper for him to stay with this beautiful girl or travel with her unless there was a wedding, but he didn't want to leave her there by herself.

"Do you want me to stay or should I leave?" he asked her.

"Whatever you want to do, you can do," she replied.

"I will build a house for you in the top of this tree," he said. "Wait for me here. When I return to my kingdom and tell my people about you, they will send a berbûk to bring you to me with rejoicing and with music."

After the youth left, two strangers—old traveling women—came down to the river. They saw a bright reflection shining across the water. They looked around but couldn't tell where it was coming from. One of the women said, "That's my reflection." The other woman said, "No, that's my reflection." They began to fight with each other and beat each other, each one claiming that the reflection was hers.

"I don't want them to fight," thought the perî. "I will tell them it's not their reflection but mine. Then perhaps they won't hit each other." She called down to them, "That is not your reflection, but the reflection of a girl sitting on a branch above your head." They looked up and saw a beautiful perî from heaven.

"Is that your reflection?" they asked her.

"Yes, it's my reflection," she said.

One of the vagabond women climbed up the tree and sat next to the perî to see if it really was the girl's reflection. She realized that it truly was the fairy's reflection, but still she wanted to cheat her. "Give me your clothes," she said. "I want to wear them to see if the light is coming from your reflection or from the reflection of your clothes."

The perî did as she was asked. Because she was from heaven, she didn't know that people could be bad. She was so clear and clean. She exchanged clothes with the woman who said, "Now let's go near the water and see if the bright reflection in the water is yours or mine." When they went near the water, the two vagabond women pushed the perî into the deep part of the river. As soon as she fell in, nature blossomed. Everything became so green and fertile. You can't imagine how beautiful and sweet it was, with flowers and blossoms everywhere.

One of the women left, but the one who had put on the perî's clothes remained. After a while, the berbûk arrived. No one even looked at the vagabond woman even though she was dressed in fine clothes. They only looked at the beautiful flowers and began to pick them. They were so unusual, such as no one had ever seen before. Everyone was happy, trying to smell all of the different flowers. The woman was angry and said, "Nobody even looks at me. What is this?" She was not very nice to them at all.

The bridal party thought she was the bride they had been sent to find. They spoke to each other, saying, "How can a padishah's son love a woman who looks like this and acts so rude. And after we brought such celebration with davul (dah-vuhl), zurna (zuhr-nah) and dancing to bring her. How will we explain when we return with someone like this? Will the Padishah's son really marry her?"

"If you are the girl we've been sent for," the people said, "why you are so mean? The Padishah's son told us that you would be sweet."

"You kept me waiting here so long that I grew bitter," said the woman.

"Why is your body bent over with age? We were told that you would be young and graceful."

"I am bent from stamping my foot on the ground and saying, 'Why don't they come to take me? Why don't they come to take me?' " the woman replied.

"Why are your lips so gnarled?" the berbûk asked.

"Because I said, 'prrrwwl, prrrwwl, prrrwwl, prrrwwl' for four days waiting for you to come and my lips stayed that way."

The bridal party conferred with each other. "What can we do?" they said. "We have to take her."

The bridal party wanted to put the false bride on the horse for the procession. But she said, "Before you put me on this horse, you have to ruin all of these blossoms and step on all of these flowers. If you don't do that, I won't come with you."

"Why do you want us to ruin these beautiful blossoms?" they asked. "This isn't your land, and no one has given you this work to do. There is no sense in this. Are these flowers doing any harm to you?"

"You have to do it," she said. "Otherwise I won't come."

They trampled all of the beautiful flowers because she was the bride and they had to do what she told them to do.

When they were ready to leave, they saw that each of their horses had given birth to a baby horse. The false bride said, "You have to kill all of these foals with a gun."

"Come now," they said, "are you an animal? Why do we have to kill them? They're so pretty, why do you want us to do that?"

"You must do it," she said. "Otherwise I won't go with you."

Eventually they had to do what she said and they killed every single foal.

While they were on the road to the castle, they saw black storm clouds coming toward them. "If you don't shoot those clouds," the woman said, "I won't go any farther."

"Who are you to tell us to shoot the clouds?" they said. "Please don't ask us to do that!" But at last they shot their guns into the clouds, because otherwise she would refuse to go any farther.

They arrived at the castle where the Padishah's son lived. As the woman dismounted from the horse, a flower fell from the circlet around her head. It was one of those unusual flowers that the perî had caused to grow. This flower became a poplar tree that grew so wonderfully and so quickly that everyone was amazed.

The Eggs of the Ancient Tree

Time passed, and the vagabond woman had a son. "I want you to make a cradle for my son out of that poplar tree outside the castle," she said.

"We will bring you a new cradle, a nice one. Why do you want to cut down this very special tree?" they asked.

"You must cut down that poplar tree to make my baby's cradle," she insisted.

At last they gave in and cut down the tree and made a cradle from it.

After a while, the woman became bored and tired of the cradle. She complained saying, "This cradle is scratching my son and hurting him when he rocks in it. I'm going to burn it." And she burned the cradle.

That same day, an elderly woman came to the castle to ask for some fire. In those days, if your fire went out, you had to go to someone else's home to get some. The elderly woman was given some of the coals from the burning cradle and she took them home with her. She put brush onto the coals to start her fire, and then she went out. When she came back, there was an egg where the fire and the ashes had been. She was in shock and said, "What's this? How can fire and ashes become an egg?" She put the egg into an empty wooden basket and left to go to another house to bring some coals again.

When she left, the egg turned into a perî. It was the very same beautiful perî, with a look that was purely from heaven. When the elderly woman came back, she saw that her house had been completely changed inside. All of the dirty dishes had been done, the rug was clean and the windows, too. Everything was perfect. She thought to herself, "Who came to this house and cleaned everything? Who helped me? Thank God!"

One day, two days, three days passed. The elderly woman again left the house, and when she returned, she saw her house had been cleaned and fixed again. "I'll hide myself and see who is coming and doing all of this work," she said to herself. The old woman hid and watched and waited. She saw a very nice girl come out of the wooden basket. This girl was so beautiful. You wouldn't even need to eat or drink; you could live just by looking at her.

"Who are you?" the old woman asked.

"Just a girl," the perî replied. "If you agree, I will be your daughter and you will be my mother."

"Why do you hide yourself?" the old woman asked. But the girl wouldn't answer her.

"Who are you?"

"I don't know," said the girl, "I just saw myself like this. Whatever you want, I will do it. You will be my mother."

The elderly woman was so happy. She didn't tell anyone about the girl.

Now every year, the Padishah's donkeys would have babies and in the wintertime the people would raise these young donkeys and keep them for him. The old woman came home one day and told the girl about this custom.

"Please, mother, bring one home so that we can raise it."

"No, daughter, we can't raise a donkey. It would be too difficult to feed."

"Go to the Padishah's house and bring me one," the girl insisted. "I will take care of it."

The old woman went to the Padishah's house and asked for a donkey. "You are a poor, old woman," he said. "How are you going to feed it?" Still she pleaded to be given one. At last the Padishah said, "Here, you can take the last baby donkey, no one else wants it." This foal was so ugly, dirty, and weak that nobody wanted to take it. It looked as if it was going to die.

The old woman brought the donkey home and told the girl that this was the last one. It was on the brink of death. "Don't worry" said the girl, "I'll put him in the stable and take care of him."

Every day the girl went to the stable and washed her hands and face before praying. When she rinsed herself in the basin, the basin filled up with food for the foal. Rich black grass and other food that is good for grazing. That little foal ate all of the grass and became so full. It was delicious food. Day after day she fed him and, when May arrived, her donkey was strong and beautiful.

That spring, the Padishah ordered his soldiers to collect all of the donkeys. The soldiers did as he told them to do, but then the Padishah asked, "Are these all of the donkeys? Are there any left behind?"

"Only the donkey you gave to the old woman," they said.

"That donkey is probably dead already. How could she have taken care of it?" said the Padishah. "Nevertheless, go and inquire about it."

The soldiers set out to the old woman's house to ask for the donkey. The girl heard that they were coming and said to the donkey, "I will never forgive you if you don't do as I say. When they take you to the Padishah's palace, sit down in front of it and don't move. Whoever comes up to you, whoever hits you, no matter if they beat you, don't move. You must not stand again until I come for you." She had given so much food and care to the donkey that she deserved complete obedience. The donkey could not speak, but it understood.

The soldiers of the Padishah came to the old woman's door. They knocked and said, "We're here for the donkey we gave you." The donkey was brought out to them and when they saw it, they couldn't believe that it had turned into such a beautiful young donkey. They took it to the Padishah's palace, but as soon as they arrived there, it sat down and wouldn't stand again. They told it to stand up. They hit the donkey; they tried to scare it. No matter what they did, the donkey would not stand.

The Padishah told his soldiers to bring him the person who had raised the donkey. "Maybe the donkey will recognize its owner and stand up." The soldiers asked the old woman to come, but the old woman told them, "The donkey will not remember me at all, it was my daughter who fed and cared for it, and she will never agree to come with you unless you line the way from here to there with featherbeds." They had to agree, and they lined the road from the old woman's house to the Padishah's castle with featherbeds.

The perî put on beautiful clothes for the journey. She put kohl (black eyeliner) on her eyes. When she arrived, the son of the Padishah was there as well. The perî gently kicked the back end of the donkey. "Hallal bê," (hah-lahl bay) she said, which means: "your debt is forgiven." And the donkey stood up. The Padishah's son saw what happened and he fell in love with this girl. The perî ran back to her house and disappeared.

One day, two days, three days, four days passed. At the Padishah's castle they were threshing wheat. Many people went to the castle to help. The perî was invited too. All of the women were talking and telling stories. The vagabond woman was at the threshing along with her baby. The perî saw her and wanted to tell everyone the story of what she had done to her, taking her clothes and taking her place as a bride. But every time the perî tried to tell her story, the vagabond woman pricked her baby with a needle. The baby cried so loudly that no one could hear what the perî said. The Padishah's son was also there, and he realized that the perî looked very familiar. He wanted to hear her story, but he couldn't because the baby cried so loudly. Every time the baby stopped crying, the woman pricked it with a needle again. It went on like that until the threshing was done.

One day, two days, three days, four days passed. But the Padishah's son had recognized the perî and knew what had happened. He sent the false bride away, never to return. The Padishah himself sent word to the elderly woman: "Whatever you want in the world will be yours if you give your daughter to my son to be married."

That is the way it happened. The old woman agreed, and a berbûk, even more joyful than the last, came to bring the perî to the Padishah's son with dancing and with music. Everyone was invited to their wonderful wedding, and it lasted for seven days and seven nights.

Note: Collected in December 2005 from a forty-two-year-old woman, Wan (Van) region, Kurmancî.

Fatima: The Kurdish Cinderella

**A girl waits for tea water to brew on top of the flames from a
tandoor oven, 2006. Photo by the author.**

*The story of Fatima, or Fato as she is affectionately called, has many of the same ele-
ments as the classic Cinderella story. Underlying story motifs such as the cruel stepmother
and the beautiful slipper lost on the way home from the dance are all the same, but the details of the tale revolve around daily life in Kurdistan. Here there is no fireplace filled with
cinders, instead, Fatima is hidden inside of the tandoor, the oven that is a deep pit in the
ground. The fairy godmother in this story is an earthy and powerful old woman, a grandmother figure called a pîrê in Kurdish. She does not wave an ethereal wand in the air to
have her magic happen, but rather pounds her walking stick upon the ground and gives
Fatima invaluable practical advice. Lêvresh is the name of the evil stepsister in the story.
Even today, when a child speaks badly or is being very naughty or cruel, parents will call
them "lêvresh." A version of this same Fatima story can also be found in Iran. This is not
surprising, as Persians and Kurds share common linguistic and cultural roots. There are
many legends and heroes that are beloved by both cultures.*

*t*here once lived a young girl called Fatima. Her father was a poor cowherd and when his wife died he married again. Fatima's new stepmother already had a daughter. The daughter's name was Lêvresh (layv-resh). She was ugly and cruel and never had a kind word for anyone. This new stepmother and her daughter were very mean to Fatima.

More trouble came because Fatima's father, the cowherd, also died. Then it was up to Fatima and Lêvresh to do his work, taking the cows up into the mountains to find pasture for them. One day it was Fatima's turn to take the cows to graze up in the mountains, and the next day it was Lêvresh's turn.

When it was Fatima's turn to tend the cows, her mother's cow always helped her in her work. It looked after the other cows and led them to easy pasture where there was a lot of good grass. But when it was Lêvresh's turn to take the cows to pasture, that same cow would lead Lêvresh and the herd to all the high and rocky places where it was difficult to walk. So Lêvresh was very tired when she returned home. Fatima's stepmother didn't like that. She decided to kill the cow and eat it.

That evening, the cow spoke to Fatima. "They are going to kill me for my meat. I will make my meat poisonous for them, but it will be good and delicious for you. I have one thing to ask of you. When I am dead, gather all of my bones and put them in the hollow of a walnut tree. Someday you may need them."

When Lêvresh and her mother ate the meat from the cow that belonged to Fatima's mother, it made them ill. The stepmother fed it to Fatima hoping that it would kill her. But when Fatima ate the meat from her mother's cow, it was very good and delicious for her.

One day, when Fatima was taking care of the cows, she came across an old woman, a pîrê (peer-ay). "Come here, daughter," said the pîrê. "Throw away the small things and eat the big things." Now Fatima knew that the old woman was referring to lice, so Fatima threw away the small lice in the old woman's hair, but the big lice she crunched between her teeth. The pîrê was pleased with this. She hit her walking stick on the ground and two kanî (kah-nee), two fresh springs, bubbled up between the rocks. One of the fountains was of red water and the other of white. "Daughter, here are two springs. Wash your face with the red water and wash your body with the white water." Fatima did as the old woman said and became so beautiful, she was like a shining light.

When Fatima came back home, her stepmother was angry with her. "How did you get to be so beautiful?" she asked. "You must be wearing makeup." She tried to scrub the beauty off of Fatima but couldn't, because it was the girl's own natural beauty shining through. Lêvresh was jealous of Fatima's beauty. "How did you do that?" she asked. Fatima told Lêvresh about meeting the pîrê and about everything that had happened.

The next day, Lêvresh went up the mountain with the cows and there was the old woman. "Come here, daughter," the pîrê said. "Throw away the small things and eat the big things." Lêvresh knew she was referring to lice. "Go away, old woman!" she said. "I wouldn't even do that for my own mother. I would never do that for you!" The pîrê nodded. She hit her walking stick on the ground and out came two kanî, two fresh springs. One of the springs was black water and one was green. "You also shall get what you deserve. Bathe in these springs. Wash your face with the black water and wash your body with the green water." When Lêvresh washed her face with the black water, her face became ugly. When she washed her body with the green water, it became rough and covered in lumps and bumps. Now all over town everyone talked about Lêvresh, because she was so ugly.

One day, Fatima went to visit the bones of her mother's cow. But when she looked into the hollow of the walnut tree, she saw that they had been transformed into a beautiful rich dress and wonderful jewelry and shoes the like of which had never been seen before—delicate golden slippers.

When she went home her stepmother said to her, "Lêvresh and I are going to a great wedding. Look!" The stepmother took a whole bucket of wheat and dumped it out on the floor. "While we're gone, I want you to pick up every single grain of that wheat."

Fatima tried to pick up the wheat. She tried to sweep it up. But there was so much, she knew she could never finish. Just then the old pîrê was passing by the door and said, "Why are you trying to pick up that wheat? Call in some hens, and they will eat up every grain." Fatima did just that and that was how she finished her work. Then she went to the hollow of the walnut tree and dressed in the beautiful gown. She put on the rich jewelry and the fine golden slippers and went to the wedding.

At the wedding everyone was admiring her. They were all so curious about her, asking her where she was from and what her tribe was, gathering around her and asking questions. Fatima danced with everyone in the line dances and threw gold on the people, which is an old wedding custom. But on her stepmother and stepsister, she threw ashes. Fatima left before the celebration ended. She put her beautiful clothes into a sack and hid them in the walnut tree. When her stepmother and stepsister returned, they saw that she had finished all of her work. But even though she had done everything as they asked, they beat her.

Time passed [The storyteller who told me this tale said here: let's not drag it out or give ourselves a headache with all of the details—time passed!], and Fatima's stepmother said, "We're going to another wedding! Here's a bucket, Fatima, and while we're gone, I want you to fill it up with your tears." They left, and Fatima tried to cry. She thought, "I'm in a bad situation. I don't even have a mother." She kept trying to think of things that would make her cry, but although she tried and tried, she could only get three tears to fall into the bucket.

The pîrê came to the door, "Fato," she called out to Fatima affectionately, "don't bother to cry. Fill up that bucket with water, add salt and mix it. If they taste it they will think it is tears." Fatima did that. She brought water, put it in the bucket, added salt, and mixed it. Then she went to the walnut tree, put on her fine clothes, and went to the wedding. Again, everyone was so interested in her. She threw gold on the people and ashes on her stepmother and stepsister and left before the celebration was finished.

On the way home, as she was crossing a brook, she slipped. Her golden slipper fell into the water and was lost there. It was so dark she couldn't find it even though she tried. She had to go home without her shoe. When her stepmother and stepsister came home, even though the bucket was full, they beat her.

In the morning, the son of the Padishah got on his horse and went riding through the countryside. His horse went to drink from the brook, but then it shied away. It saw the gold reflection of the shoe and didn't want to go near the water. The son of the Padishah looked to see what was disturbing his horse, and saw something shining in the water. He went into the brook and pulled out the beautiful golden slipper. He took it home with him and said to his father, "I have found a beautiful golden slipper. I will have it tried on the foot of every girl. Whomever this slipper fits, even if it is the daughter of a cowherd, I will marry that girl." The Padishah said, "Whatever you wish, my son."

The Padishah's servants traveled everywhere, but no one they found could fit into the golden shoe. They asked, "Isn't there someone who hasn't tried it on yet?"

"Only the two daughters of the cowherd," they were told.

They went to the cowherd's house, but the stepmother wouldn't let Fatima come into the room. Lêvresh tried to fit into the shoe, but she couldn't wear it. "Isn't there any other girl here?" they asked. The stepmother said, "Oh, you don't have to bother with her, she's nothing." Still they insisted, and Fatima was brought in. When Fato, put on the shoe, it was a perfect fit. Word was sent back to the Padishah that the one whom the slipper fit had been found. And so he sent his bridal party, the group of young women that they call a berbûk, to Fatima's house to dress her as a bride and bring her to the castle.

Before the berbûk arrived, the stepmother put Fatima into the tandoor oven and placed a heavy iron cover on top so that she couldn't escape. She put her own daughter Lêvresh in the middle of the room seated upon the carpet.

The berbûk entered the house and Lêvresh was introduced to them as Fatima, the bride. The stepmother went to prepare some tea, and while she was gone a cat came into the house and said, "Fatima is in the tandoor and Lêvresh is sitting on the carpet." Then it left. The people didn't understand what the cat said and kept talking to Lêvresh as though she were the bride. Then the dog called down through the smoke hole in the roof. "I respectfully wish to say that Fatima Xatûn (khah-toon), that is, Miss Fatima, is in the tandoor, Lêvresh is on the carpet!"

One of the women in the bridal party said, "What are the cat and the dog talking about?" Just then the rooster came in and crowed, "Fatima is in the tandoor!" "Let's look in the tandoor," they said.

They took off that heavy iron cover and there was Fatima sitting in the tandoor and quietly knitting her socks. They pulled Fatima out, put Lêvresh into the tandoor, and dragged the heavy iron cover back over it. Then they piled sheep's manure on top. They didn't wait for Fatima's stepmother to return, they dressed Fatima as a bride, placed her on a horse and had a big celebration as they left. With dancing and with music they made the procession.

Lêvresh's mother came back and didn't see her daughter. She thought Lêvresh had been taken by the bridal party, and she cried and cried. But when she pulled the iron cover off the tandoor, she saw Lêvresh sitting in there. "Oh my daughter, my naughty daughter, what are you doing here?" Lêvresh told her mother how Fatima had been taken by the berbûk and she had been put into the tandoor.

The story goes that they took Fatima to the palace, and for seven days and seven nights they had a wedding party.

Time passed, and Fatima was so beautiful and nice that God gave her a baby.

One day Fatima's stepmother decided to go and visit her. She made a potion from grains of wheat and put the kernels into a comb. The stepmother said to Fatima, "My daughter, I would like to wash your body." "Mother, I'm clean and don't need a bath," Fatima replied. The stepmother insisted that she be allowed to wash her, but when she scrubbed Fatima's body and combed her hair Fato turned into a bird and flew away. The stepmother left Lêvresh in Fatima's place and came back home.

In the evening, the son of the Padishah saw that the baby was crying and he asked Lêvresh, whom he thought was Fatima, "Why don't you nurse the baby?" "The baby won't take any milk," said Lêvresh. Two or three days passed, and the son of the Padishah understood that this was not Fatima. He knew there was something wrong, but he didn't know how to find out what had happened.

Meanwhile, his servant Osman was putting together a pile of hay to feed the animals. A bird flew down and asked him, "Is Lêvresh at home?" He said, "Yes, she's at home." "How is the baby?" asked the bird. "The baby is not good," he replied. Then the bird cried.

Osman went to the son of the Padishah and told him the story about the bird and what it said. The Padishah's son disguised himself as Osman and returned to the same place. The bird came down from the sky and asked him, "Is Lêvresh at home?" The son of the Padishah said, "Yes." The bird asked, "How is the baby?" He said, "The baby is not good." And the bird cried.

The Padishah's son called the bird closer. Little by little the bird came down to his feet. He caught hold of the bird and stroked its head. As he petted the bird, the grains of wheat fell out of its head, and the bird became Fatima once more.

Lêvresh and her mother were brought to the palace and tied to two horses. One of the horses was very thirsty and the other was very hungry. One went toward the water and the other toward the food and those two were torn apart. From then on, everyone was happy. And that is the end of the story.

Note: From versions collected in May 2005 from an eighty-one-year-old man, Bitlîs region, Kurmancî, and from a fifty-three-year-old woman, Agirî (Mount Ararat) region, Kurmancî.

The Zay Tree and the Tay Falcon

*T*hey say that long ago there was a king who had three sons. It happened that the king went blind in both eyes, and no matter how the physicians treated him, they had no success. The astrologers looked into the matter and said, "If the zay tree and the tay falcon[1] can be found for him, he will regain his sight, provided the falcon goes to the top of the tree and sings for him."

When asked where the tree and falcon were to be found, the astrologers answered, "They are in a country far, far away in the city of the fairies, beyond Mount Qaf,[2] guarded by demons. They will be very difficult to obtain, if at all possible."

The people said, "The king has three sons. If this zay tree and tay falcon can't be found by them, they ought to die." The sons set out courageously, each one in a different direction and each wanting to be the one to get these things. The youngest brother, who had a different mother from the other two, chose a way for himself all alone. Only God knows how far he went before he reached the outskirts of a city, where he looked and saw that the city was surrounded by a great wall with a huge gate in the wall. When he approached the gate, the guards stopped him and said, "Every stranger who comes to our city must first go before the king. After that he may go about his business." Thus he was taken before the king of the city.

"We ask a few questions of all who come to our city," the king said. "If they can answer them, we reward them and let them go about their business. If they can't answer, we cut their heads off. You see that tower? We have made it of the skulls of such people."

"Your majesty," said the youth, "I am ready to answer any question." "Good," said the king. "In the behavior of living things does nature or nurture take precedence?"

"Your majesty," answered the youth, "nature takes precedence."

"No," said the king. "It is not so, and I'll prove it to you." The king rang a bell, and immediately two cats came into the room, each holding a candle. They lit the candles and then began twirling around a basin of water. Then they extinguished the candles and took down the basin of water, which had been placed on a slightly elevated place.

The king turned to the youth and said, "Well, did the cats' mothers and fathers know how to do this or not?"

"Obviously they did not," answered the youth.

"Just so," said the king. "They learned it by training. Now, have you lost the bet or not?"

The youth was obliged to confess that he had lost.

Now the king ordered those around him to take the youth away and cut his head off, but along the way the youth said, "Please, don't kill me. I am a king's son, and I have a lot of money with me. I'll give it all to you and be on my way. How is the king ever to know?" They agreed and took his money. The youth left the city and fled. How far he went nobody but God knows, but he came to a mountain cliff in which he found a cave. Since he had a sword and some arrows, he decided to venture into the cave. Once inside, he looked and saw a woman sitting there—a beautiful woman without equal. You'd say her neck was made of crystal, and if she had swallowed raisins, you could have seen them as they went down. As soon as the woman saw the youth, she started weeping. In astonishment the youth said, "Why are you weeping? I am a human being like you. Are you a prisoner here?"

"Yes," she said, "I am a prisoner here, but I am weeping for you because now the demon will come back, and if he sees you here he'll tear you to pieces."

"If you help me," said the youth, "I'll hide myself until the demon comes. You keep him occupied, and I'll kill him with this sword and rescue you."

"Fine," said the girl. "I'll do as you say. Go, hide yourself."

It wasn't long before the demon came, roaring and rumbling, into the cave. The girl stood in front of him and began to serve him. The demon was surprised and said, "Why is it that today you come before me? It's obvious you've got something up your sleeve."

"Inside this cave in the midst of the mountains, what could I be up to and what could I have up my sleeve?" she replied.

Then she flitted around the demon to distract it and make it turn its back on the youth. Then the youth attacked with his sword, and as he severed the demon's head from its body, something fell out of the demon's hands. The youth looked and saw that it was a box. He picked it up and took the lid off. Immediately two slaves stood before him and said, "What do you command?"

"Who are you?" he asked.

The slaves replied, "We are slaves of anyone who possesses the box, and we will do whatever he wants."

"Good," said the youth. "Now go into the box, and I'll tell you when I want you." Then he put the lid back on the box, put it in his pocket, and said to himself, "They will come in handy."

Then the youth said to the woman, "Now I have to go get the zay tree and the tay falcon. I don't know how long it will take me, and I don't know whether I'll come back or not. It's up to you: you can go or stay and wait for me here until I come back. I have freed you. Now it's your choice." "I will not leave here until you return," she said. "All my treasures and goods are here. I'll stay and wait for you."

The youth then bade her farewell and left. How far he went nobody but God knows, but he came to the outskirts of a city. When he got near the city gate, two guards stopped him and said, "We'll take you before the king. Every stranger who comes to our city has to go before the king. After the king questions him and he answers, either he is allowed to go or his head is cut off."

The youth said, "I am not going into your city, and I am not going before the king either. I am going to go on my way past here."

"You can't," they said. "You have just come." However, it was of little use. The youth would not submit. The news was taken to the king, and he dispatched five guards who said, "If you don't come we'll kill you!"

The youth stood his ground and fought with them. Invoking the name of God, he killed all five of them. Then a large army came out of the city to attack him. The youth took the box and removed the lid. Immediately the two slaves appeared before him and said, "What is your command?"

"Defeat this army for me!" he said. As soon as his order was spoken, the two black slaves fell upon the soldiers and laid them low left and right. Defeated, the army withdrew into the city. Helpless, the king sent a vizier and a wise man to the youth to find out what he wanted and to grant it in hopes that he would leave them alone.

"Of what religion are you?" the youth asked.

"We are fire-worshippers," they said.

"I am a Moslem," he said, "and if you will convert to Islam, I'll leave you alone." Thus the king became Moslem, and the people all followed him in converting to the religion of Islam. Then the king asked, "What are you looking for and what are you after?"

"I am after the zay tree and the tay falcon," the youth said.

"Who can reach them?" the people said in amazement. "They are surrounded by demons. But if you are determined to go, you will find them in such-and-such a country on such-and-such a mountain and in such-in-such a place."

"My son," the king said, "let me send an army with you."

"Your majesty," the youth said, "that is not necessary. I'll go alone. Until now I haven't known the way."

Then he said good-bye and departed. How far he went only God knows, but with inquiry he came to the country in which the zay tree and tay falcon were. He searched for a long time until he came across a high mountain. There he took out the box and removed the lid. Immediately the two slaves stood before him, saying, "Master, what do you command?" "I command you to go to the city and find me a lot of pegs, a steel stake, and several hammers," he replied. The slaves disappeared, and in the twinkling of an eye they brought him what he needed. They hammered the stakes into the mountain, and the youth scaled it. "Bring me a rope and lower me down," he said. The slaves immediately brought some rope and lowered away.

The youth looked and saw that it was a large palace. On every side horses were tied, and in front of them were placed bones so that they would constantly be hungry and neigh and keep the demons from going to sleep. In the same way there were many dogs tied up, and they had straw and barley so that they too would always be hungry and bark to keep the demon guards of the zay tree and tay falcon from going to sleep.

The youth took the bones from the horses and gave them to the dogs, and he took the hay and barley and gave them to the horses, and both the dogs and the horses fell silent and began eating. Then the youth saw that the door to the room where the zay tree and tay falcon were was hung with bells, and if he touched them they would fill the room with their jangling. Therefore he ordered the slaves to bring cotton, and he stuffed the bells with it.

Then, when he was convinced that all the demons were asleep and nothing would wake them, he reached out, opened the door, and went inside. He looked, and there lay the queen of the fairies asleep and covered with a silken curtain. The zay tree was placed to one side, and the tay falcon was perched atop, and it too was asleep. Next to the queen of the fairies were placed four lamps, one at her head, one at her feet, and one on either side. Then he changed the places of the lamps: those that were high he lowered, and those that were low he raised. Then he looked carefully at her face. She shone like the full moon. He couldn't help himself. He kissed her, and immediately the place he had kissed became a blue spot on her cheek. Then he put the falcon in his pocket, picked up the tree, and was about to leave, but his legs wouldn't carry him. He returned to the queen of the fairies, raised the silk curtain, and looked. She had on a pair of trousers with forty knots. He untied thirty-nine of the knots, but the fortieth was tangled, and he couldn't untie it, so he left it as it was. Then he ordered the slaves to pull him up to the top of the mountain, and from there he got down with the help of the stakes. Then he ordered the slaves to find horses, and like the wind they went to the cave where the girl was waiting. There he put down the zay tree and tay falcon and said, "I am going to be gone for a few days. Let these remain here in your keeping until I return," he said. "Then we can leave together."

The prince then went to the city where he had escaped death with such difficulty. Traversing the distance in a few days and nights, he came to the city gate, and there the guards stopped him and, just as before, took him before the king.

"My son," said the king, "where have you come from?"

"Your majesty," he replied, "I've come from a far distant country."

"Our custom in this city is to ask a few questions of every stranger who comes to our city," said the king. "If he answers correctly, we reward him. If a correct answer is not given, we cut his head off. Did you notice that tower? It had been made of the heads of such people."

"Your majesty," replied the youth, "I am ready."

"Fine," said the king. "In the behavior of living beings, does nature have precedence or nurture?"

"Your majesty," he answered, "nature has precedence over nurture."

"No," said the king, "it is not so. Now I will prove to you that nurture comes before nature. I will have two cats come. They will each light a candle and twirl around this basin of water. Then they will put the candles out and take the basin down from its elevated place. Obviously their mothers and fathers have not taught them this." The youth asked the king for permission to be excused, and he went outside and ordered the slaves to bring him two mice, which he put in his pocket.

When he came back, the king rang a bell. It wasn't long before a door opened and two cats, each holding a candle, came in. They lit the candles and began turning around the basin of water. Straight-away the youth turned the mice loose, and as soon as the cats saw them, they left the candles and began chasing the mice.

"Your majesty," said the youth, "it happens that nature has precedence."

"Yes," said the king, "you are right, and you have won the wager. Now let me reward you."

"Of what might your reward consist, your majesty?" asked the youth.

"My reward is myself," he said, and there and then he flung off his regal garments and his head covering, and lo and behold he was a beautiful woman. "Now I'll marry you," she said.

The youth was stunned, but then said, "I'd kill you before I married you, because my two brothers were looking for the zay tree and tay falcon, and they must have come to this city and you must have killed them."

"Don't kill me just yet," she said, "for many people have escaped by paying money, unbeknownst to me." Then, at the king's command, all the prisons were searched, and it turned out that they had not been killed but were in chains. They were brought to their youngest brother, and all three rejoiced in the sight of each other.

Then the king said to his courtiers and to the people of the city, "Until now I have been your king, and nobody knew I was a woman. Now I have decided to go with this youth, and you can choose a new king for yourselves." All the people praised her for this.

Then they departed. Along the way the youth told them that he had found [the] zay tree and tay falcon. Then they went to the cave, got the zay tree, the tay falcon, and the woman, and set out for their own country.

The two brothers were very disturbed by their youngest brother's fortune, and they were jealous. Along the way they spoke together, saying, "If we go like this, our youngest brother having done everything so courageously and heroically, we will be dishonored." Therefore they made a plot to kill their brother and each marry one of the two women. Then they would write to their father telling him they had obtained the zay tree and the tay falcon themselves.

Along the way, they stopped somewhere to rest, and then they said to the youngest brother, "Dear brother, let the women go ahead, and we'll follow them on our good horses and catch up with them. Just now we have some things to discuss amongst ourselves, and we don't want anyone else to hear us." The youngest brother, who was completely pure of heart and would not have conceived that after all the good things he had done for his brothers they could harbor any rancor for him in their hearts, did as they said and sent the women on ahead. Then the two elder brothers treacherously attacked him, stabbed him, and threw him into the river. Then they set out after the women.

Let us follow the fate of the youngest brother. His brothers had stabbed him and thrown him into the water, thinking he was dead, but he wasn't dead, for there was still a scant breath of life in him. As the blood trickled from his body, the water turned red and flowed downstream to a nearby mill. When the miller looked, he saw that the water was red, so he followed it upstream until he found the body drenched in blood lying in the water. He reached out, pulled him in and looked. There was still a bit of life, so he took the youth home and tended to him. After a time the youth recovered and told the miller what had happened.

Now let us follow the brothers. When they caught up with the women, they asked them where their youngest brother was. "He's behind," they said, "but he'll be along in a while." After several nights and days of traveling, they reached their own city. They took the zay tree and the tay falcon to their father, but the falcon wouldn't sing. They then doubted whether they were the real zay tree and the tay falcon, so an astrologer was called in.

The astrologer examined them and said, "They are the real zay tree and tay falcon, but the tay falcon will only sing when the person who has caught it stands next to it. Therefore it is clear that the youngest brother found it, and these two brothers have tricked him and done away with him."

In the meanwhile, after the youth's wounds had healed, he decided not to leave but to stay and live with the miller because, after all his heroism and manliness, his brothers had been so cruel to him. Now let us go to the city of the fairies and find out what was going on there. When the queen of the fairies woke up after her forty-day and forty-night slumber, she looked around and saw that the zay tree and tay falcon were no longer there. Furthermore, the bones had been thrown to the dogs, and the hay and barley had been put in front of the horses, and they were all eating silently. The queen got excited and angry and beat her demon and fairy sergeants, saying, "Fly into the sky and scour the earth from east to west, and find the zay tree and tay falcon for me. If you don't I'll kill you!" And so the demons and fairies dispersed left and right and searched the earth until they discovered them in the city of the blind king.

The queen of the fairies wondered who had done it, but no one dared to own up to it and confess. "This can only have been done by a champion hero," said the queen of the fairies. "If only I could discover who did it, I would give him the best reward." Once this was known, lots of people claimed to have done it, but the queen of the fairies demanded proof, and no one had any. Like others, the king's two sons had been rejected. Word spread everywhere that the queen of the fairies had sent out a swarm after the zay tree and tay falcon and had come herself to reward the person who had taken them away. Therefore the youngest brother got up and went to his father's house, and as soon as he arrived the falcon began to sing and the father's eyes were healed. Putting his arm around his father's neck, he told him of his adventures, how he had obtained the zay tree and tay falcon and what his nasty brothers had done to him, that they had tried to kill him but God had not let it be done, and how the miller came to his rescue.

"My son," the father said, "the queen of the fairies has come, and she wants to reward the person who has done this deed, but she demands proof."

The youth went to the queen of the fairies and said, "I took the zay tree and the tay falcon."

"All right," she said, "what is your proof?"

"First I stuck a steel pole in the mountain, and then I got on it and let myself down with a rope. There I took the bones from the horses and gave them to the dogs, and I took the hay and barley from the dogs and gave them to the horses. I stuffed the bells on the door with cotton, and then I went in. I changed the lamps on all four sides of you, and I kissed you on the cheek, which became a blue mark. Then I took the tay falcon, which was asleep on the zay tree, and put it under my arm, and I picked up the tree and made off with them."

Then she freed all the demons, saying, "You are free to go where you will. I remain here as this youth's wife."

Then the youth sent for his brothers and said, "I didn't have to say that I performed the task by myself, and I could have married each of you to one of the women, but you acted shamefully and did me a great wrong. Now, for my father's sake, and for the sake of the viziers and counselors, I forgive you. Each of you may marry one of the women."

They lowered their heads in shame. Later the youngest brother married the queen of the fairies, and they all lived happily ever after.

Notes: "The Zay Tree and the Tay Falcon" was collected by Mohammed Tofiq in Iraqi Kurdistan between 1980 and 1990. This story first appeared in *The International Journal of Kurdish Studies,* 13(2) "Kurdish Folktales" ©1999. The translation is by Wheeler Thackston of Harvard University. Reprinted here with permission.

1. Zay and tay do not have specific meanings in the Kurdish language.

2. In the Islamic tradition, Mount Qaf is the mythical mountain at the edge of the world. It is the place where the visible and invisible worlds meet. Here many magical beings including fairies and jinn (genies) have their dwelling places.

𝕬 Sister with Seven Brothers

A group of girls were sitting together one day, making lace.[1] As they were working, one of the girls passed gas loudly. This was not considered polite at all and everyone wanted to know who did this.

"I swear on the life of my brother it wasn't me!" said one girl.

Another girl said, "I swear on the lives of my two brothers it wasn't me!"

A third girl said, "I swear on the lives of my three brothers it wasn't me!"

And so it went until at last it came to the seventh girl. She didn't have any brothers to swear upon, she didn't even have a father, so she swore on her mother's hair. Everyone laughed at her for that and made fun of her. "It must have been you that passed the gas," they said.

She went home crying.

"Why are you crying, my child?" asked her mother.

"Mother, I'm crying because in our family there is only you and me. There is no one else."

"Oh, but that's not true. Didn't you know that you have seven brothers? You've never seen them because they live in another country far, far away."

"Mother," said the girl. "I want to visit them. How can I get there?"

"It's a very long way. You cannot get there on foot, but, if you would like, I'll make you a donkey out of dust and on its back you can travel very far and very fast."

So her mother fashioned a donkey from the dust, and the girl climbed onto its back. "No matter what you find along the way, even if it be gold or jewels, don't get off your donkey to pick them up," her mother cautioned. "If you do, the donkey will melt into the earth again."

The girl set off. She didn't travel very far before she saw gold shining on the ground. She got off of her donkey to pick it up and the donkey became a pile of dust. She returned to her mother and told her what had happened, and her mother again made for her a donkey from the dust. She cautioned her not to stop for anything along the way. The girl set off, but this time she saw money lying along the road. When she got off her donkey to pick it up, the donkey sank back into the earth once more. This time when she returned home, her mother told her that this was the last donkey she would make, so the girl should be very careful not to stop at all.

This time the girl did not even look down. She traveled until at last she came to a big house. She went in and, as no one was around, she cleaned the whole house, made delicious food and set out seven plates. Then she hid herself in a big crack in a pillar.

In the evening, her brothers came home from hunting. The house was clean and there was fresh food on the table. They wanted to know who had done this, whether it was a spirit, a genie or a mortal. They decided that the brother who had seven eyes should keep watch to find out who had helped them.

While he slept, the brother with seven eyes kept two of his eyes open and the rest of his eyes closed. He saw a girl coming out of a crack in the pillar and cleaning the house. He alerted the rest of the brothers and together they caught her. The girl explained that she was their sister who had journeyed all this way to meet them. They were happy to see her, but they cautioned her to be very careful. "There is a giant, an ogress, who lives nearby," they said. "Make sure you never go near her castle. She is very dangerous."

Every day the seven brothers would go to the forest to cut wood and every day, after their sister had finished her housework, she would go up to the flat roof of the house and spin wool into thread with her teshî (teh-shee), her wooden spindle.

One day, the girl annoyed the cat that lived in the house. When she did, it urinated on the fire and put it out. The girl knew she needed embers to start the fire again, but she didn't know where to get them. She went out looking for a place to get coals, and at last she arrived at the only place nearby. It was the castle of the ogress.

The ogress was away that day, but her seven daughters answered the door. "We can give you fire, but you have to know that our coals are counted. Our mother knows exactly how many should be there and she'll know if you take some." "Still," said the girl, "I must have them."

"Well then be careful. Don't show yourself to our mother and leave quickly."

The girl left quickly with her embers. As she was leaving, she tripped, and thread from her teshî became tangled in some branches. The thread unraveled behind her as she ran.

The moment the ogress entered her castle, she said, "I smell the smell of a human!" The daughters told their mother that a girl did come, but that she lived far, far away. "We'll see how far she may be," said the ogress, and she left in search of the girl.

The ogress found the thread and followed it all the way to the house of the seven brothers. The gate was closed and locked. "Open the gate to me!" she demanded. But the girl refused. The monster pleaded with her saying, "If you won't open the gate, at least put your finger through the keyhole so that I can suck on it. I am weak and dying from hunger." The girl hesitated and the ogress said, "If you don't do as I say, I'll kill whoever comes to this house, no matter how many there may be." The girl didn't want her brothers to be killed, so she put her finger through the keyhole. After the ogress sucked on it, the girl turned pale and fell down in a faint.

Every day when the brothers were out hunting, that monster would come back. The girl let the ogress suck on her finger and, when she was finished, the girl would faint.

One day, the brothers came home and found their sister unconscious on the ground. They realized that something was terribly wrong and, the next day, they hid to see what the problem was. After a while, the ogress came up to the house and began to suck on the girl's finger through the keyhole in the gate. The brothers jumped out of their hiding place and killed the monster.

Now that the ogress was dead, they decided to go to her castle and see what was there. When they went in, they discovered the ogress's seven daughters. Each brother married one. The brothers warned their sister to be careful, "Our wives are the daughters of a monster. They might kill you or deceive you. Be very watchful of anything they give you or ask you to do."

The daughters of the ogress made the girl work for them. They made her work very hard. One day they told her to go out to the pasture to drive the cows and sheep away. "The animals are eating all of the grass on the pasturelands and we need to save it to harvest for the winter." The girl went out to the field and shooed away all of the cows and sheep. It took a long time and when she returned home she was very tired and thirsty. The daughters of the ogress put a piece of hair from their mother's skin into a pitcher of water and left it out for the girl. She drank that water and after that, the hair from the demon's skin caused her belly to grow bigger every day.

The wives complained to their husbands, "Look, your sister has become pregnant. You have to do something with her. Take her away from here and kill her." The brothers told the youngest brother to take their sister into the forest and get rid of her.

The next day, the youngest brother took his sister to a forest far away. He told her that he was going to cut wood and wanted her to come with him. It was a long journey and when they stopped, she was tired and laid down under an oak tree to rest. The brother didn't have the heart to kill her, so he collected acorns and tied them together with string. He hung them from a tree and, when the wind blew, they hit each other and made a sound like someone chopping wood in the distance. He did that so that his sister would not know that he had left. When the girl awoke she found that her brother had abandoned her there to die. She was so upset that she cursed him, saying:

> *"May a snake's spine pierce your foot as you walk upon the land,*
> *No medicine will cure you till I heal you with my hand."*

The sister had to travel far to find a place to stay. At last a villager took pity on her and brought her to his home. He thought that she was pregnant, but she said, "I'm not pregnant, I have snakes in my stomach and that is my problem." The villager brought out pickled vegetables that had been in a big clay jar for seven years. He opened the jar and held it in front of her nose so that she breathed in the strong smell of the pickle juice, and snakes came out of her mouth. They left her stomach because they hated the smell of this acid juice. After that the girl was healed.

Time passed and she married the villager. One day as she was baking bread, she spotted a visitor coming toward the house. He was limping, and she recognized that it was her youngest brother. He didn't recognize her at all. She asked him why he was limping, and he told the story of how, when he was walking home one day, he stepped on a snake. "When I did, the snake's spine went into my foot. I have looked everywhere, but no one can help me."

"Let me help you," she said. "I might be your cure."

His foot and leg were very swollen. She took a long needle and pierced the swollen wound. She got out all of the bad infection and also the backbone of the snake. It looked like a comb. She gently wrapped her brother's foot and it began to heal. Afterward, she took him into her house. He stayed with her, and, in time, she told him the whole story of who she was, how he had abandoned her and how she had found a new life. In time she and her brothers and her mother were reunited, and they all lived long and prosperous lives.

Notes: Collected in 2005 by Yuksel Serindag, Cewlig region, Dimilî, translated by Yuksel Serindag. Additional parts of this story were collected in January 2007 from Saadat Fidan, village of Kello, Sivas region, Kurmancî. An additional version was collected in January 2007 from a seventy-year-old woman, Wan (Van) region, Kurmancî .

1. Kurdish girls can spend hours making beautiful and intricate lace items. They make these special borders and decorations for the new home they will have once they get married.

Legendary and Heroic Figures

Aqil taca zêrîn e: li serê her kesî nine.

Wisdom is like a crown: it doesn't cap everyone's head.

—Kurdish Proverb

Leaping over the flames is a common sight at a Kurdish Newroz.

Kawa and the Birth of the Newroz Celebration

One of the most important Kurdish holidays is Newroz (nehw-ruhz) an Indo-European New Year's festival occurring on March 21, the time of the Vernal Equinox. It is celebrated in Kurdistan, Iran, Afghanistan, India, and various countries of Central Asia. For the Kurds, the celebration of Newroz has taken on special, even political, significance in recent years. Associated with the legend of Kawa the blacksmith, Newroz is seen as a time to unite and celebrate victory over oppression. A young woman heard the following story when she was a child. It was told to her by her father, and after telling the story to the children, he then lit the Newroz fire. There are many versions of the Kawa legend, this one has a lovely simplicity to it.

*T*hey say that once there lived a cruel king by the name of Dahak.[1] He terrorized his people and only looked after his own well-being. It happened that on top of each of his shoulders a great sore appeared, and out of each of these sores a snake's head emerged. Gradually everyone came to know that this wicked man had a serpent growing out of each shoulder. Wisemen and those who cure all disease were summoned to see if they could rid the king of this painful aberration. They told him that the only way to appease the snakes was to kill young village boys and girls and feed their brains to the serpents. "If you do this," the king was told, "the snakes will slowly disappear."

The king commanded his soldiers to bring two young people to the palace every day. He told his cook to have the young people killed so that their brains could be prepared as food for the snakes. Day after day, week after week, month after month this continued, but the snakes did not disappear. When they were fed, for a little while the pain would cease, but the next day the king's torment returned, and he again ordered more children to be sacrificed.

The people were terrified for the lives of their young ones and went to Kawa, the blacksmith, asking him for help. Kawa was a very strong and clever man; he secretly went to the palace and convinced the cook to spare the youths' lives. His plan was to deceive the king by feeding the serpents the brains of sheep instead. The young people who were saved were

taken to the remote mountains and kept hidden there. To keep the plan a secret, not even the parents were told that their children were still alive.

Kawa told these young people that someday he would kill the evil Dahak. "To let you know that I have succeeded and that we are free of this tyrant, I will light a great bonfire. When you see this, light your own fires on the mountaintops so that everyone will know that the day of our freedom has come."

Kawa did make a plan to kill the evil king and, with the help of the cook, he stole into the castle one night. He made his way to the king's chamber, and with one great swing of his blacksmith's hammer, he was able to kill the evil tyrant and his snakes.

That same night, the Spring Equinox, the young people who had grown up in the mountains saw a sign. A huge fire was burning right beside the palace. When they saw it, they knew that at last the evil king had been destroyed. On every mountaintop, those that Kawa had rescued made their own fires, dancing around them and jumping over the flames in joy.

It is said that the Kurds are descended from the children who were saved during the reign of Dahak. To this day they still live in their beloved mountains and, every year on March 21, they light fires and celebrate the triumph of freedom over tyranny. Newroz is not just the beginning of a new year for the Kurds; it is the beginning of a new age.

Notes: Collected in May 2006 from a twenty-five-year-old woman, Mardin region, Kurmancî.

1. Prince Sharaf, the Kurdish emir of Bitlîs, does not mention the figure of Kawa but gives an overview of this legend in *The Sharafnâma: or the History of the Kurdish Nation* written in 1597 (translated by Mehrdad Izady). In this translation, the snakes growing out of Dahak's shoulders are snake-like veins enlarged by cancer. Dahak (spelled Dahhak in *The Sharafnâma*) is referred to as the king who "occupied the throne of Persia and Central Asia (Eran and Turan) and the rest of the world after Jamshid." (This quote taken from the Prologue to the *Sharafnâma*, English translation and commentaries by Mehrdad Izady [Costa Mesa, CA: Mazda, 2005], p. 28.)

Sultan Mahmud, Heyas, and the Mysterious Black Knight

This is one of many legends told about Sultan Mahmud and his wise advisor, Heyas. The Sultan attributed his success to the fact that he never did anything without first consulting Heyas, and Heyas never misled him or gave him wrong advice.

*E*very few years, Sultan Mahmud would travel around the kingdom looking after the well-being of his people. Our story begins with such a journey, with Sultan Mahmud, his wise counselor Heyas, and the entire retinue setting out accompanied by a great deal of music and merriment.

After a week of walking, walking, walking, putting one foot up and one foot down, the Sultan ordered camp to be made so that everyone could have a few days of rest. He went to take a nap in the shade of a cave and asked Heyas to guard him from any danger while he slept. As Heyas was standing guard by the sleeping Sultan, a snake came out of a hole right by the Sultan's head. Heyas drew his sword to kill the snake, but in the same moment the snake slithered back into its hole. The noise of the sword awakened the Sultan and what did he see above his head? There stood Heyas, brandishing an unsheathed sword and poised as if to strike him. Angered and alarmed, the Sultan ordered his guards to arrest Heyas.

Now when the Sultan awoke, he heard Heyas say, "Alas, it went." The Sultan didn't know what to make of Heyas's words nor did he give him the opportunity to explain, and his most reputable advisor remained in captivity for the rest of the long journey until the Sultan and his men returned home.

Upon reaching the palace, Sultan Mahmud consulted with his ministers and wisemen to determine what kind of punishment should be given to his chief advisor. They argued long and hard over this sticky business, but at last they decided that because of his long service to the Sultan, Heyas's only punishment should be to be exiled from the city.

Heyas gathered a few belongings and left, wandering the countryside until at last he arrived at a watermill owned by an old miller and his wife.

"Who are you and where are you going?" they asked.

"My name is Karim," he replied, "and this is my story. I was once the shepherd for a rich man. One day while the sheep were grazing a wolf attacked and killed one of the lambs. Because I could not prevent it, I was sent on my way and now I have no home and no work."

The elderly couple had no children of their own, and they asked Heyas to be their son, to live with them and help them with their work. Heyas agreed.

Meanwhile, after Heyas left, a strange and terrible thing began to happen in the city. Every night, as it grew dark, a black knight would ride through the streets wearing a heavy veil over his face so that no one could identify him. Each night he knocked upon a different door and when someone opened the door, he slew them. Night after night this terror continued until, in alarm, the Sultan called all of his ministers and counselors together, asking them to find a solution to the problem. After much deliberation they said, "Sir, no one can solve this dilemma except Hassan Meimeni."

Now Hassan Meimeni was Heyas's father and the Sultan's former advisor. He was one hundred and fifteen years of age—so old that he had to be carried in on a stretcher. The Sultan asked his former advisor who the Black Knight was and how he could be defeated.

"Your Majesty," said Hassan, "no one can solve this riddle except my son."

The Sultan objected, "Heyas has been exiled. We don't even know where to find him."

"I'll help you find him," said Hassan. "Simply give each household in your kingdom a newborn lamb and enough money to feed it for one year. But tell them that in a year's time, the lamb must be returned to you weighing no more than it did when they received it."

"That's impossible!" said Sultan Mahmud. "How can a person raise a lamb that doesn't grow?"

Hassan Meimeni smiled and said, "That part won't be difficult for Heyas. He is my son, and I know how clever he is."

The Sultan agreed to the plan and gave each household a lamb on the condition that in one year's time it would still weigh the same amount. When the old miller received his lamb, he felt very sad because he didn't know how to fulfill the Sultan's request. Heyas asked him, "What's wrong, father?" The miller told him the story and how hopeless it would be to try to raise the lamb as the Sultan wanted. Heyas told him not to worry. "Let me take the responsibility of caring for the lamb. I will find a way. You'll see."

Heyas went to a cowherd who passed by with his cattle every morning. He asked the cowherd to bring him a wolf cub in exchange for two liras. The cowherd readily agreed and the very next morning brought him a wolf cub he had found in the mountains. Heyas put the wolf cub and the lamb together in a shed, and the lamb was so frightened of the wolf that it never grew.

One year passed, and all of the lambs were brought to the royal palace to be checked and weighed. The old miller brought his lamb as well and, to everyone's amazement, it passed the test. Officials questioned the old man, asking him how he had achieved this. At first he wouldn't tell them, then at last he admitted that he didn't know how it was done, because it was not he, but his son, Karim, who had solved the problem. The Sultan and his followers set out for the watermill to see if the old man's son, Karim, was indeed Heyas.

When Heyas saw the Sultan coming toward him, he shouted out, "At last it came!" The Sultan recognized Heyas and, dismounting from his horse, embraced him warmly. "Can you tell me why you cried out, 'At last it came!' when I arrived?" asked the Sultan.

"Your Highness, do you remember that when you saw my sword raised above your head I said, 'Alas, it went?' I said that because the snake that was about to strike you had just disappeared. Now that you have asked me, I can tell you that the absence of that snake was the only reason that I was accused of disloyalty. Therefore I said, 'Alas, it went.' Your arrival here proves to me that you trust me again. Therefore, I called out 'At last it came,' meaning your good faith."

The Sultan asked Heyas for his help in confronting the mysterious Black Knight that was terrorizing the city. Heyas agreed, asking only that he be given forty days' time.

A few nights later, while Heyas was reading, he heard a knock at the door. Immediately he put on his armor and opened the door. There was a black knight mounted on a black horse. The knight motioned to Heyas to follow him, and Heyas got on his horse and rode with him out of the city.

As they were riding, Heyas said to the knight, "You usually kill the person who opens the door to you. Why didn't you kill me?" The knight replied, "I killed all of the others because none of them were ready for me. For over a year they have heard about people being slain when they opened their front door at night. Still, they didn't prepare themselves. But you were ready, and came out like a brave man ready to face any danger." By now they had arrived at a deep cave.

The knight motioned to Heyas to dismount and enter the cave, and they both went inside.

Heyas said to the knight, "Tell me your story. Why have you committed all of these crimes?" Before any answer was given, the knight pulled off the heavy veil covering the face and Heyas could see that this knight was really a beautiful young woman.

"I am Banaz, daughter of the Mîr of Ardalan,"[1] she said. "The chief minister of our land wanted me to marry his son, but I refused. I said that I would only marry the one who could defeat me in a wrestling match. The chief minister agreed to a contest, thinking his son would be strong enough to defeat me, but he lost the wrestling match in the first round. Ashamed and enraged at the defeat of his son, the head minister sought revenge. He gathered his forces, overthrew my father and put him in prison. I escaped and have been searching for a way to win back my father's kingdom ever since."

"Your story is truly tragic," Heyas said, "but what amazes me is that you came to our land and killed our people. Why did you come here at all?"

"The fame of Sultan Mahmud is widespread. I have heard of his power and of his wise advisor whose name is Heyas. I was looking for some brave fighters among your people to help me regain my lost kingdom. But, unfortunately, every time I knock on a door, the householder comes out in his pajamas instead of his armor. I would like to ask Sultan Mahmud for fifty brave soldiers. The forces of the head minister are cowards and will not resist us. You seem to be a brave and intelligent man. Please, will you be my emissary to the Sultan? I'm sorry, I don't even know your name."

"I will tell you my name tomorrow at the royal palace," Heyas said. "Come there in the morning and we will speak to the Sultan together. Good night, Banaz."

When Heyas left, all he could think of was this beautiful and spirited woman. He would like to have her as a wife himself! After sleeping a few hours, he got up, ate his breakfast, and rushed to see the Sultan. On seeing Heyas, the Sultan asked, "Why are you here so early?"

"Your Highness, I came to ask you a favor. You asked me to solve the problem of the knight who was killing our people."

"Yes, that's right. Did you find him?" the Sultan asked.

"I certainly did, but the knight is not a he but a very attractive she. Indeed, I have fallen in love with her and wish to marry her."

The Sultan was stunned, "Are you telling me that you want to marry my enemy?"

"She is not your enemy, your Highness. It only appears that way," and Heyas told the story of what he had learned the previous night.

Banaz was ushered into the divan, the room used for receiving guests, and she bowed to the Sultan. She did not notice Heyas standing next to the throne. "Your Majesty, I am Banaz, the daughter of the Mîr of Ardalan."

"The Mîr of Ardalan?" the Sultan interrupted her. "Why, he is my friend. What has happened to him?"

Banaz told of her father's imprisonment. After listening to her, the Sultan said, "You should be punished for the crimes you have committed. However, I will forgive you for two reasons: first, you are a courageous woman, and second, your father is a virtuous ruler and does not deserve to be in prison. But I will only help you on one condition, and that is if you marry my advisor, Heyas." With a twinkle in his eye, he motioned to Heyas who was standing by his side.

Banaz looked at the man standing beside the Sultan and recognized him as the one who had traveled with her last night. She was startled to learn that this man was also the Sultan's famous advisor, Heyas. "I have heard of Heyas. His bravery and wisdom are well known even as far as Ardalan and I admire him for those traits," she said. "But I made a vow that I would only marry the one who could overcome me in a wrestling match. If Heyas would marry me, he must fight and win."

A wrestling match between Heyas and Banaz was arranged for the following day. Heyas had assumed that he would win easily, and it was true that his love for her gave him extra strength and speed, but it was not enough, for she was a strong and skilled athlete. Still, in the end, love won out, for as Banaz wrestled with Heyas, she fell more and more in love with him. He was young and handsome and she couldn't stop thinking of his courage and his wisdom. Though she was strong, she allowed him to win so that she could have him as her husband. She declared defeat, and a great wedding was held.

The marriage celebration lasted well over a week. When at last the festivities were finished, the Sultan provided Banaz with a detachment of soldiers. Together she and Heyas marched to Ardalan and overcame the forces of the evil minister. They released her father from prison and put him back on the throne of Ardalan.

In the end, they all lived happily with no more wrestling matches or murders. They had many children that were all as wise as Heyas and as strong as Banaz. The story ended and I came back empty-handed.[2]

Notes: Collected by Leeya Thompson in 1993 from Sheikh Tinue Berzinjî, Soranî. Contributed from Leeya Thompson's unpublished manuscript: *Winter Tales: A Collection of Kurdish Folktales*, ©1996.

1. Mîr (meehr) means emir, prince or ruler. Ardalan was, at one time, a semi-independent Kurdish state with its capital at Sine, now in Iranian Kurdistan. Ruled by the family known as Ardalan, it existed from approximately 1168 to 1867.

2. "And I came back empty-handed" is one of the typical endings to a Kurdish story.

Rawchî the Ḫunter

The Goranî (goh-rah-nee) story of Rawchî (rawcî is the Kurdish word for "hunter")
originated sometime during the second half of the seventeenth century C.E. Mustafa Dehqan
collected versions of this tale in 2000–2001 in Iranian Kurdistan to create the following
story. In particular, it draws upon the telling of Muhemmed Sediq, dengbêj (story-singer),
from Hewraman. Mustafa Dehqan relates that those who recite the legend believe it to be
based upon historical occurrences. Many of the tellers said that the powerful Turkish
prince Sencer (sehn-jehr), referred to in this story, is an explicit reference to Sultan Sencer,
a Seljuk King of Iran. Whether or not this is proven to be true, the legend of Rawchî remains
the only extensive record that exists of the habits, attributes, equipment, and companions of
this Kurdish hero whose reputation extended far beyond the Kurdish emirate of Hewraman[1]
and throughout the rest of Kurdistan.

*J*t came to pass that in the Kurdish territory of Hewraman the Turkish king passed
away. Now at that time, there were a hundred princes, any of whom would be ea-
ger to step into the position of ruler. But in the end, the rulership of Hewraman and the rest
of Kurdistan went to the most powerful of all the Turkish princes, Sencer (sehn-jehr).

Sencer appointed many commissioners to help him rule. Emin, a Kurdish hero, was
one of them. Emin had no son to carry on his name, but he gave a special place in his home
and in his heart to his servant, Kawe (kah-weh), whom he loved as though he were his own
offspring. Emin had no idea that Kawe was descended from the noble Kurdish family of
Kirmaşan (kihr-mah-shan).

One night, Emin had a dream. In it, he saw his servant, Kawe, seated upon a red horse.
In the dream, a crowd was gathered around Kawe bowing low to him and blessing him.
Emin wondered what it could mean and invited the sages and interpreters of dreams into his
presence. He told them of the vision he had seen. The sages interpreted his dream by saying,
"Either the person you saw in your dream, or one of his sons, will become the ruler of
Hewraman." When Emin heard this, he summoned Kawe and questioned him about his her-
itage. He asked him who his family was and if any of his ancestors had been rulers before.
Kawe told him his secret: that he was descended from the noble Kurdish family of Kirmaşan
from the region of Goran. Emin was delighted with Kawe's reply and gave him his daughter, Banûcuan (bah-noo-jooahn), in marriage. Rawchî (rahw-chee) was their firstborn child.

As Rawchî grew, Emin could see how clever he was and he thought his dream might have had some truth in it. He treated Rawchî as though he were his own son.

When Rawchî reached the age of seventeen years, news reached Sencer that his commissioner Emin had a son who excelled in learning, wrestling, and riding. Sencer wrote a letter asking that Rawchî be sent to him as company for his own sons. Sencer was king of Hewraman, powerful and absolute, and it was improper for Emin to ignore his command. So Rawchî was sent to Sencer's palace and, in time, he became more victorious and warlike than Sencer's own sons at polo and wrestling.

One day, Sencer went hunting along with his sons and with Rawchî. A boar happened to be running in the desert and Rawchî and Ülek (oo-lehk), the eldest son of Sencer, pursued it. Rawchî closed in on the boar and shot an arrow into it with such force that the arrow pierced through its belly and all the way up to its eyes. The boar died instantly. Sencer didn't witness the event, but when he approached and saw how the boar had been killed, he was astonished at the skill and power of the deed.

"Who shot that arrow?" he asked.

"I did," Rawchî replied.

Ülek contradicted him saying, "No, you did not, because I did."

At this, Rawchî became angry and said to Ülek, "It isn't possible to take away the skill and heroism of another by using tyranny and lies. There are many wild boars here. Let's try a second time."

Sencer was offended that Rawchî spoke that way to his son. After that incident, he wouldn't even allow him to ride on horseback. He sent Rawchî to work in the stables saying, "Don't speak to the princes again. And take care that you stay with the horses and cattle. Don't leave to go hunting or to attend the college of learning." Sencer was jealous that Rawchî's heroism exceeded that of his son's. But it was especially cruel of Sencer to deny Rawchî the studies that he loved.

Sencer had in his service an accomplished maiden, whom he regarded with greater respect and affection than any other maiden who served him. One day, while Rawchî was seated by the horse stalls, this same maiden passed by. When she saw him, she was captivated by him. She went to see him often and soon fell in love. Every night, when the unfortunate Sencer went to sleep, the maiden would secretly visit Rawchî, stay with him until the dawn, and then return to the palace. She became Rawchî's spiritual helper.

One day, Sencer invited into his presence the sages and astrologers and asked them the following question, "What do you see in the planets and the signs of the zodiac regarding the condition of the people of the world, and regarding myself?" The chief of the sages and astrologers replied, "It is clear that any male servant who runs away in the next seven days will attain kingship and be victorious over his king." The maiden was there when the sages made their prediction and later told Rawchî what they had said. He resolved to leave at once.

Rawchî saddled two of Sencer's horses. He seated himself on one and the maiden on the other, and they set out on the road, riding with great speed. That same morning, Sencer called for the maiden, but she was not to be found. The stable-master came in and said to Sencer, "Rawchî and two of your steeds are missing." That was how Sencer became aware that one of his maidens must have run away with Rawchî. The chief of the astrologers said to Sencer, "It is clear that Rawchî has fled and is now on the road heading deeper into Kurdistan. If he is not overtaken within seven days, it won't be possible to capture him afterward. Immediately Sencer prepared five thousand men and, led by one of his sons, these armed men set out to capture Rawchî.

Rawchî continued on his way. Several of the inhabitants of Hewraman who had been distressed by the treatment they had received from the Turkish princes placed themselves, their wealth and their property at his disposal, pledging their loyalty. Later, when he reached the place they call Şetl (shehtl), a magnanimous hero by the name of Memo, who had himself escaped from the hands of Sencer, came personally to Rawchî, along with his sons and many Kurdish soldiers and heroes. He approached Rawchî, took an oath, and gave him confidence with these words, "As long as I live, I will remain loyal to you." Rawchî prepared an army.

Rawchî battled with Sencer and his sons, eventually destroying the entire army of the latter, seizing their wealth, property and horses, and settling himself in Hewraman. There he collected Kurdish soldiers in large numbers from Kirmaşan, Merîwan (mehr-ee-wan), Sine, Sablax (sah-blakh), also known as Mahabad, and other regions and came himself to fight with Sencer. Sencer sent for soldiers and provisions from different villages of Turkestan but Rawchî gained success. He defeated Sencer, whose entire wealth and property fell into his hands.

Afterward, Rawchî marched toward different frontiers and fought many battles with the principal rulers of the territory of Kurdistan. In the end, he was able to bring the whole kingdom of Kurdistan under an absolute monarchy and the head rulers of different frontiers under his submission. He demanded tribute from them and made the kingdom of Hewraman more embellished, more efficient, and more famous than any before.

Notes: Collected and translated by Mustafa Dehqan, Hewraman, Iranian Kurdistan, Goranî.

1. Hewraman is located along the Sîrwan River and the present Kurdish provinces of Kirmaşan and Sine in Iranian Kurdistan.

The Legend of the Shahmaran

According to a ninety-year-old woman from Wan (Van) region, Kurdish houses are often adorned with a picture of the Shahmaran to guard against the evil eye. The design might be embroidered, painted or, as is done in the Mardin region, etched onto fine metal trays.

Once, long ago, there lived a historian, a learned man whose name was Darya. One day he said to his wife, "Most of my life has passed and I feel that my death is very near. You are going to give birth to our child soon, and, if you give birth to a boy, my last request is that his name shall be Jamisav. He will grow to be a wise man and a good person. I beg you to honor my last request."

On the day Darya died, his wife gave birth to a boy. She named her son Jamisav and when he reached the age of ten, she sent him to school to become a learned man.

At school, Jamisav couldn't understand anything; he wasn't a good student at all. So his mother took him out of school and sent him to try carpentry, but there also he couldn't succeed. Next she sent him to a tailor, but he couldn't learn that skill either. It continued to go this way for Jamisav. He grew up, but he never learned anything.

When he was fifteen years old, he went to his mother and said, "Mother, I tried my best. I have gone here and there, but still I haven't learned anything. It can't go on like this. I have to provide food for us to eat or we are going to die of hunger. If you buy me a cart and a donkey, I'll go to the forest and collect wood, and that's how I'll earn a living." Jamisav started cutting and selling wood and, a few weeks later, he had enough money to buy another donkey and cart. Two friends joined him to work with him and they shared that donkey and cart between them.

One rainy day, he and his two friends went into a cave on the side of a mountain. Jamisav picked up a stick and began scratching a circle in the ground. At first, he was just aimlessly digging, but then he started digging deeper and deeper into the ground. He dug a

---

round hole. To his surprise, at the bottom of the hole was a large flat stone. It looked as though it were covering something.

"Come, help me!" he said to his friends. "Maybe together we can lift the stone. I think there's something underneath."

When they lifted the stone, they saw that it was covering a well, a well that was filled to the brim with honey. They were all very happy. They said to each other, "God gave us a good well. Now we don't have to collect wood anymore. The treasure is here." They started collecting honey and pouring it into their meşken (mesh-kehn),[1] their leather sacks. They sold their honey at the market.

Day after day they went back and forth, collecting and selling honey until there was very little left. They sat by the well getting ready to divide the profits. It had been agreed that Jamisav would take half of the money, and the other half would be divided between his two friends.

Now at the very bottom of the well, there was still a small amount of honey left. "There's still some honey left down in the well," said Jamisav. "Who's going to go down and collect it?" His friends were uncertain. They looked at each other and then said, "Jamisav, you go down and collect it." Jamisav felt a sense of foreboding. "I am my mother's only son," he said, "and we're very poor. If I go after the honey, please don't leave me down in the well."

"If you collect all the honey that is there," his friends replied, "after we take the honey out, we promise we'll pull you out, too."

Jamisav went down into the well. He started collecting all the honey that was left and sending it up to his friends. After a while, his friends called down to him, "Is there any honey left in the well?" "No," he replied. One of the friends said to the other one, "Let's cover up the well and leave him down there." The second friend said, "No, we shouldn't do that. He's been our best friend."

"Listen to me and don't be stupid. If we get him out, he's going to take half of all of the earnings. He'll get twice as much as you or I. He's going to be rich and we're going to be poor. Let's leave him down there. We don't owe him anything."

They closed the stone back over the well, and Jamisav was shut in.

Jamisav prayed, "Xwedê (kweh-day), God, you created everything on this earth. Now I appeal to you hoping that you will do something for me. Please rescue me from this place."

After he finished his prayer, he saw a scorpion coming out of a hole in the side of the well. It came closer and closer. Jamisav was frightened and crushed the scorpion under his foot. Then he examined the place where the scorpion had emerged from the wall. He saw that there was a faint bit of light coming from somewhere. He took a knife out of his pocket and started to make the hole larger. He dug until there was a passageway big enough for a person, and then he crawled through.

When he emerged on the other side, what he saw was beyond description. How could it be that behind the wall of this well there existed a whole other world with a beautiful palace and rich land? But there it was. He looked around, but there was no one to be seen. No human, no demon, no genie; it was completely empty. The palace had two sleeping areas, one up and one down. He lay down on one of the beds and was so tired he fell asleep.

Suddenly there came a lot of noise. It was a sound louder than thunder. Jamisav woke from his sleep, startled awake to an indescribable sight. Before him stood the most beautiful woman he had ever seen. She shone like an angel. He couldn't take his eyes off her. He wanted to always gaze upon her. Soon, he was surrounded by many other angelic beings. He told them the story of his friends' betrayal and begged them to help him get out of the well.

"We can't help you do that," they said, "but we will make you our honored guest."

"If you won't help me to leave, then I'm not your guest, I'm a captive here."

He pleaded with them so long and so eloquently that they called forth the ruler of that realm to speak with him. That was the legendary Shahmaran with the head and torso of a woman and the body of a snake. The Shahmaran glowed with light.

"Take me out of the well, please!" said Jamisav.

"Don't ask me to do that," said the Shamaran, ruler of all the snakes. "If I leave this well, no matter where I go or what I do, I will never escape from the grasp of human beings. They are hunting me always for my knowledge and they will kill me in order to get it. If I set you free, they will find out where I live and they will behead me."

The angelic beings pleaded for the youth, begging the Shahmaran to set him free, to which the Shahmaran replied, "Don't you accept what I say, that if I set him free I will be beheaded? Human beings are deceitful. I don't trust them at all. If I take him out, in the same minute he will betray me and I will die. Listen, Jamisav, to my stories and you will understand why I say this and why I cannot take you out of this well."

The Shahmaran began spinning tales both wonderful and terrifying. Jamisav couldn't tell where one story ended and the next began. He listened, and he forgot his longing for home. On and on the Shahmaran wove her stories. She told tales about her magical knowledge and of how she was once deceived by a crafty human. This evil man forced her to use her powers so that he could try to steal the magical ring of Silêman (sih-lay-mahn), or King Solomon. Solomon's ring gives its owner the ability to create or destroy. She told of her eventual escape and of the difficulties of the way. Once or twice Jamisav interrupted and pleaded to be taken home, saying that his poor mother needed him. But then another tale would begin, even more marvelous and more instructive than the last, and he would be spellbound once more. As time wore on, Jamisav was filled with so much grief and worry for his mother that he said to the Shahmaran, "Don't you have a heart? You're killing me by keeping me here. My mother needs me."

"Very well, I will let you go," said the Shahmaran. "I can see that you will never be happy here. But listen to me, because I am going to advise you. In the center of your city lives the Padishah and he is very sick. He has a minister who is a magician and I am sure that he will be out looking for you. He knows that the fluid in my body is the medicine that will cure the Padishah. Because he is a magician, he will know what signs to look for to find the one who has met the Shahmaran. He will be able to find you and question you. Whatever they tell you about me, whatever they say, whatever they do; don't tell them anything. Keep your encounter with me a secret. But if they make a move to cut your throat and kill you, tell them the truth. They will ask you to lead them here. When you arrive at the well, I will come out and they will kill me. They will cut off my head, and boil my meat. When they boil it, three different liquids will rise to the surface. One of the fluids will be yellow, the next will be green, and the final one will be white. When this happens, my son, when the white fluid comes out, drink that white fluid. After you drink that, you will be wiser than anyone in the world. Give the green fluid to the magician, and he will die. But the third fluid, the one that is yellow, rub it on the body of the Padishah and he will be cured. When you cure the Padi-shah, he will be so grateful that he will give you his daughter in marriage. As his son-in-law, you will be the one who will be the king when he dies. Do not forget all that I have told you. Now, let's take you up to the world again."

Jamisav was lifted out of the Shahmaran's kingdom and he found himself standing outside of his own home in the middle of the night. He knocked on the door.

"Who's knocking?" his mother said.

"Mother, I am the one knocking. It's your son."

"That's impossible," she said. "My son is dead."

Still she opened the door, and when she saw that her son was alive, she hugged him.

Meanwhile, the Padishah's minister was searching for anyone who might have seen the Shahmaran and knew where she lived. After a week of searching, he heard that there was a certain person named Jamisav who, no matter how far he traveled, would never take a public bath. He knew this person must have seen the Shahmaran and said to the Padishah, "Have your guards find this Jamisav and bring him to me."

The guards searched far and wide. They found Jamisav and brought him to the Padi-shah.

"Take off your clothes," said the Padishah's minister.

Jamisav took off his clothes, and everyone saw that there were spots all over his body. The minister, who was also a magician, told everyone that these spots were a sign meaning that someone had been in the company of the Shahmaran. The Padishah said, "My son, tell me where the Shahmaran lives." "I don't know," said Jamisav. They tried many cruel meth-ods to get Jamisav to speak, but he wouldn't tell them anything. At last they threatened him saying, "My son, we're going to cut off your head if you don't tell us."

Now remember, the Shahmaran had told Jamisav, "If they tell you they are going to kill you, tell them the truth. Show them where my palace is."

Jasmisav guided them to the well where the entrance to the land of the Shahmaran lay hidden. The magician took out his book and started reading spells. As he recited those magi-cal words, the Shahmaran emerged from the well, alone. The magician went to the Shahmaran to grab her and she said, "Don't come near me. You are dirty. Let Jamisav hold me." Jamisav wrapped the Shahmaran in a cloth, placed her under his arm, and brought her to the Padishah's palace.

"Don't kill me," said the Shahmaran to all who were there. "If you cut off my head you will be lost forever."

But the magician struck the Shahmaran and cut off her head. Then he started boiling her flesh in water. From this he extracted three fluids, one yellow, one green, and one white.

"Jamisav, which of these fluids do you wish to drink?" asked the magician.

"I will drink the green one," said Jamisav.

Although the Shahmaran, had told him to drink the white fluid in order to gain all knowledge, he wanted to drink the liquid she said was poisonous. He was so distraught that he had betrayed the Shahmaran that he wanted to die.

"If you want to drink the green fluid, that must be the one which gives all knowledge. I will be the one to drink that one," said the magician.

The evil magician drank the green fluid and died. Jamisav was left with the white fluid. When Jamisav drank it, he gained all knowledge. The third fluid, the yellow one, Jamisav rubbed all over the Padishah's body. Because of this, the Padishah was completely cured and without a blemish on him. The Padishah was very grateful to Jamisav and wanted to reward him. He gave Jamisav his own daughter to marry, and they had a big wedding and many children and their children had many more children. And I wish the same for you.

Notes: Collected in May 2005 from an eighty-five-year-old man, Erdîş (Erciş/Van) region, Kurmançî, translated by Sardar Jajan.

1. Meşken are bags made out of the hide of a whole lamb. Often they are used to churn cheese, butter, or even yogurt.

Rustemê Zal

In the Kurdish storytelling tradition, Rustem is an important legendary figure. He is so strong and brave that he is often called the "Kurdish Hercules." Also claimed by Persians as their folk hero, Rustemê Zal or Rustem, son of Zal is celebrated in both cultures.[1] There are countless legends told about this "pelewan," meaning a knight, champion, or noble warrior. This tale is but one small chapter of his story.

Note: The length, detail, and subject matter of this tale makes it unsuitable for most read-aloud situations or for younger audiences. Nevertheless, this gripping legend is an important example of the longer heroic tales traditionally told in Kurdish culture, and, as such, it gives insight into the fearless stoicism and bravery that is part and parcel of the Kurdish ideal of the pelewan—the warrior-hero.

*I*n the time of Rustemê Zal (ruh-stehm-ay zahl), God bless the listeners and those who are present, the world was divided into two parts. One part belonged to the Turans and the other part to the Aryans. They had different kings and were enemies against each other. Rustem was an Aryan. He was the hero that the Turans especially wished to defeat.

Once, when Rustemê Zal was on a great journey through the world, his horse became lost. Now Rustem's horse, the piebald colored Reshbelek (rehsh-beh-lehk), was no ordinary horse, and he was determined to find it again. He searched until he found it in the possession of one of his enemies, a man called Shergir, a wrestler who was one of the Turans. Rustem told Shergir that he wanted his horse back. "I will give it to you, but only if you will stay with my daughter for ten days," he said. Rustem agreed and stayed with his daughter for ten days, after which he left and went home. God gave a son to that young woman, and Shergir named the boy Zorav, which means strong and difficult to overcome.

One day Shergir and his grandson Zorav were out working in their field. Shergir saw Esfesyar's (ehs-feh-syahrs) men coming to collect the tax. They walked up to him, right through his field and Shergir said, "Why are you walking through my field and damaging my crops? Why don't you walk on the road instead?" The men answered, "We will walk wherever we want to. We are Esfesyar's men and he is king here."

Zorav picked up a spade, and killed six of the seven men. The only one who survived ran straight back to Esfesyar and told him that Shergir had a boy with him that was so powerful he overcame six men. Esfesyar called his advisors and commanders together and asked them whether Shergir's family had ever had such powerful men or wrestlers in it. His commanders analyzed the nature of the fight and told him that this youth could not be from Shergir's clan; he must be from the clan of Rustemê Zal.

Esfesyar called Shergir to the court and asked him "Who is this boy that killed so many of my men?"

Shergir said, "He is my grandson, Zorav."

"Is this grandson your son's child or your daughter's child?" asked Esfesyar.

"He is my daughter's child," Shergir replied.

"Who's the father of that boy?"

"Rustemê Zal is the father."

"Then I don't need you, Shergir, I need your grandson, Zorav. Bring him to me."

" I will bring him to you on one condition," said Shergir, "and that is that when he is old enough, he will be given your daughter to wed."

"That may serve us both well," said Esfesyar, and he sent Shergir away.

Esfesyar said to his commanders, "I'm going to keep this boy, Zorav. I will feed him and raise him to fight Rustem. "That's right," said his commanders. "No one can beat Rustem except someone from his own clan." Zorav was brought to Esfesyar, and he was fed on meat, rice, and mey (may), a type of wine, until he became very strong.

Esfesyar was true to the promise he had made to Shergir, and when Zorav was old enough, Esfesyar gave him his daughter to wed. They lived together for one month. God gave a son to that woman, and that child grew up to become a strong and powerful man just like his father, Zorav, and his grandfather, Rustemê Zal.

Zorav was trained daily in the art of battle by Esfesyar's men and one day, Piran, the head commander, told Esfesyar that Zorav was now a pelewan (peh-leh-wahn), a warrior. He had become such a powerful wrestler that it was impossible to overcome him.

"Bring him to fight Rustemê Zal soon," Piran said, "because if he finds out he is Rustemê Zal's son and joins up with his father no one will be able to beat them after that."

"He knows he's Rustemê Zal's son," said Esfesyar, " but he's never seen his father so he won't recognize him. You're right though; we should bring him to fight Rustem before he knows more."

They took Zorav to the arena used for tournaments. They put up their tents and prepared for the fight against Rustemê Zal. They didn't tell Zorav who his opponent would be. Rustem arrived at the arena and the match began. For three days and three nights, they rode against each other in the arena, but neither one of them could gain victory. At last Zorav said, "The horses are exhausted. We're enemies, you and I, but what have the horses done to be involved in our fight? Let's dismount and wrestle on the ground." Rustem replied, "I was going to say the same thing to you, but I thought you would say, 'He's a bit heavier than me.

That's why he's requesting that.' All right, let's wrestle on the ground." They released their horses and began wrestling on the ground.

It was a difficult fight. Whenever Rustem gets into trouble when fighting, he says, "God is great!" Then he becomes seventy times more powerful than his enemy and his enemy becomes seventy times weaker. When Rustem said, "God is great!" he was able to throw Zorav to the ground. He took out his sword and ran it into Zorav's body.

"You have slain me, but how can you beat my father?" Zorav said.

"Who is your father?" asked Rustem.

"My father is Rustemê Zal."

"No! I have destroyed myself!" Rustem cried out.

He took Zorav into his arms and ran to find help.

The Aryans mourned and the Turans celebrated the incident because Rustem had mortally wounded his own son.

Rustem went to his father Zal and asked him to give him medicine to cure Zorav, but Zal said he had no medicine for such a serious wound. He told Rustem to go to the holy man, Kerim Khesrew. "Go there, and remove the sword from Zorav's body. If that doesn't kill him, ask Kerim for medicine." He went to Kerim Khesrew, and there he pulled out the sword and asked for medicine. Kerim said, "The wound is too deep; there is no cure for it."

"Then I'll pretend that Zorav was never my son," said Rustem.

Thousands of Rustem's people came to celebrate his victory over a wrestler from the Turans. However, Rustem was deeply troubled because he had caused the death of his own son.

When Zorav's son was grown, he was a very strong man. Rustem didn't know he had a grandson and, this time as before, Esfesyar prepared the youth to fight him.

Esfesyar brought the youth to the arena to face Rustem. Rustem swung his mace at the youth and missed him. Then his grandson strongly swung his mace, and it broke Rustem's arm. Rustem didn't let anyone know that his arm was broken but said, "That's enough for today. We're going to take a rest now." He returned to his tent, very concerned.

"What's wrong with you?" said his father, Zal. "You've had more serious injuries in the past and you never worried this much."

"The wrestler who fought me today is going to destroy our family," Rustem replied. "He is so strong. I have never seen such a fighter. Can you search and find out about his ancestry? What family does he come from?"

Zal, Rustem's father, was a great fortuneteller.

"As far as I can see, he is one of us, though I don't know how he is related," he said.

Rustem was worried about the next day's fight and asked if there were any powerful men within the family to go against this pelewan for him. His own son Felemez said that he would go, but Rustem told him that he didn't have the strength. "I'm your son," Felemez said. "And I want to fight him."

Rustem prepared Felemez to fight. His son was not a very strong or a very heavy man, but he was skillful and clever and he used these techniques when he fought. Rustem coached him and gave him his own horse, Reshbelek, to use in the fight.

The next morning Felemez got on Reshbelek and went to the arena. When he arrived, Zorav's son said, "Where is the wrestler I fought yesterday?"

"I am here!" said Felemez.

"No, that wasn't you," said Zorav's son. "You're a little thing and I'm going to kill you!"

"You're in a dream and you don't even know what's going to happen," Felemez taunted him back. "I'm going to kill you!"

They began fighting on horseback. Felemez swung his mace and it wrapped around Zorav's son binding him. At the same time Zorav's son swung his mace, and it tied Felemez tightly. They tried to drag each other in opposite directions, spurring their horses. Felemez bound himself to the horse, Reshbelek. Reshbelek was so strong that when they spurred their horses it pulled the other horse over. Zorav's son fell off and was dragged back toward the camp of his enemy. He tried to catch onto a rock to stop Reshbelek from dragging him, but Felemez ordered the horse not to stop and Reshbelek continued on, pulling both the boulder and the man. "Whatever you do," shouted Felemez, "even if you hold onto a mountain, you won't be able to stop me from taking you to our camp." Felemez captured him and took him to his father's camp where he was imprisoned.

Zorav's wife heard what had happened to her son and, hiding her identity, she came to Zal's house to be as a mistress to him, earning the trust of all around her. She waited patiently for an opportunity to release her son from prison. During this time, Rustem traveled to a specialist for the treatment of his arm. At the end of forty days, his arm was healed and he headed home. As Rustem was headed home, the youth's mother was on her way to the prison. She untied her son, and they left together.

After one or two hours, Felemez and the prison guards realized that this woman had freed the prisoner, and they began to pursue them. Felemez saw them and shouted out, "Hey, pelewan! You're our prisoner. When prisoners escape they shouldn't travel with their mistresses." When Zorav's son heard this he stopped. At the same time, Rustem arrived on the scene. When Zorav's son saw Rustem he said, "That's the wrestler who fought me on the first day!" Rustem said to everyone, "Stand back, I'm going to fight him and I don't want anyone to interfere."

Everyone stood back, and Rustem and the pelewan started wrestling. Zorav's son had been in prison for forty days. He hadn't eaten enough, and he was very weak. But Rustem had been fed very well while he was under treatment, so it took him only twenty minutes to throw his grandson to the ground. Rustem pulled out his sword to kill him and the youth's mother cried out, "You have destroyed your offspring once, don't do it twice."

"Why do you say that?" said Rustem. "Who is this youth?"

"This is your grandson, the son of Zorav," she replied.

Rustem picked his grandson up off the ground. He kissed him and lifted him up onto his shoulders. The Aryans held a great celebration for the reuniting of Rustem and his grandson. But the Turans were very upset, saying, "Now that Rustem and his grandson are together we may be destroyed."

There was a jubilant celebration in front of Rustem's house and all of the Aryans at Rustem's command came. Three of the most important Aryan leaders—Givû Gûhdar (gih-voo gooh-dahr), Tûzê Nevrashah (too-zay nehv-rah-shah), who was married to Rustem's daughter, and Mêran Kabilî (may-rahn kah-bih-lee), Rustem's nephew—arrived late, each of them accompanied by fifteen hundred pelewan fighters. It was a show of strength and pride that they claimed loyalty from so many brave warriors. Rustem came out to greet them but then immediately went back inside. At this, all of the fighters hung their heads and looked down. They were speechless. They thought, "What happened to Rustemê Zal? Why didn't he want to see us?"

The commanders went to Rustem and said, "We have so many people with us that have come to see you and you're not welcoming them. You're not interested in them. Why?"

"Why don't you talk to us?" said Tûzê Nevrashah. "We're all waiting for you to speak."

"What can I say?" said Rustem. "You're welcome to join in the celebration, to eat your food and then go back where you came from. What I need cannot be done by you. I will have to do it."

"Rustem," they said, "it's true that whatever you say, you can do. But tell us what it is. You are free to speak."

"You know that Esfesyar owes us something," said Rustem. "Since the day that he caused me to kill my own son, that wound has been in my heart. I will go to the highlands they call Mêrgezer (mayr-geh-zehr), where there is a lot of grass and fresh springs. I will fight Esfesyar there."

The fighters knew that Mêrgezer was Esfesyar's favorite highlands; he always took his herds there in the warmer weather. They were frightened and looked away. They wouldn't even meet Rustem's eyes.

"Why don't you say something? You made me speak and now you just hang your heads. Are you coming with me to Mêrgezer or not?" Rustem asked.

"Rustem," said Mêran, "if you will allow us, we're going to consult with each other. Whatever we agree upon, we will tell you."

Mêran, Givû and Tûz, Rustem's three most important commanders, went off by themselves to talk. They consulted together saying, "If we go to Mêrgezer, we may never return. We may all be killed there. So let's make our own plan. We know that Mêrgezer is a twenty-five-day walk from here. Let's send two of our men to see if warm weather has arrived, and to see if it's a suitable place for the fight or not. It will take them two months to go and come back and, in the meantime, something else may happen and we'll be free of this obligation."

When they returned, Rustem said, "Have you three made your decision?"

"Yes," they said. "This is what we think. It's spring and it may not be the best time to go to the highlands right now. So we have decided to send two of our men to Mêrgezer to see if the snow has melted and to see whether the time of belekevî (beh-leh-keh-vee) when the streaks of grass appear, has arrived or not.[2]

"Are you going to deceive me with this?" asked Rustem. "I'll send my own two men to see if belekevî, has come. They will go and return in a few days."

"It's your decision," they said.

Rustem told two of his men Zavare (zah-vah-reh) and Gûrgîn (goor-geen) to go and see if the snow had melted in the sunny places and whether the climate was suitable or not. They said, "With pleasure!" and rode their horses up to the highlands. A journey of twenty-five days, it took them only three. They examined Mêrgezer. They took out their spyglasses and wrote everything down. When they returned, they presented their findings to Rustem. "We've never been in a more beautiful place in the world," they said. "We should go there."

Rustem told his commanders, "If you need swords, there are plenty of them in the shops. If your mace is light, it can be made heavier. If you need arrows, you can get them. If your horses are not good, ours are good and we'll exchange them for you. You have fifteen days to get ready. Once you are prepared, we'll move."

Fifteen days passed. During that time each of them prepared fifteen hundred fighters. Rustem himself had two thousand fighters, and they all moved toward the highlands. They went up to Mêrgezer and camped there. It was so beautiful. There was a cool kanî (kah-nee), a spring, there, and Rustemê Zal set up his tent by it. The others also put up their tents and released the horses. Flowers were everywhere—so many wonderful scents it was like a paradise.

Meanwhile, among the Turans, Esfesyar was speaking with one of his men, the guard of the highlands. He asked him why no one had gone up to Mêrgezer yet. "If you haven't been there this year, maybe someone else has settled there and is grazing their animals and finishing up the grass. Go and look, and make sure it's still ours."

The man set out and went to the high peak of Hîmevanê (heem-eh-vah-nay) Mountain. From there he could see everywhere. He looked down on Mêrgezer with his spyglass. He was shocked at what he saw. There were so many horses that the manure was knee deep. There were thousands of pelewans and wrestlers. Some were hunting, some were walking by the kevî (keh-vee), the deep snow that takes the longest to melt. He saw a great warrior down on the plain. The hair on his head was down to his knees in length. He was so powerful and so big that when he went into his tent, he couldn't even fit inside. His arms, as well as his legs from the thigh down, fell outside of his tent. When Esfesyar's man saw such a powerful warrior, he dropped his spyglass in shock. He picked it back up as quickly as he could and went back home.

Piran, Esfesyar's chief commander, knew the highland's guard very well. He noticed that he went straight home and seemed filled with fear. As the day grew late, Piran said to Esfesyar, "The inspector of the highlands hasn't come to speak with us."

Rustemê Zal

"Maybe he hasn't returned yet," Esfesyar said.

"No, he's back," said Piran.

Piran sent one of his servants to tell the highland's guard to come to speak with them. But the message came back that the highland's guard was ill and couldn't come. Esfesyar said, "All right, if he's ill, he's ill." But Piran said, "No, it's not that he's ill. I think he saw something at Mêrgezer. I think he's afraid." Again the request was sent to the highland's guard to come, and again the request was refused. Piran said to his men, "That guard is a simple pelewan. How can he reject my invitation? I have the authority. Go and tell him to come a third time. If he doesn't come, I'll have him brought here by force and give him a beating as well." So Piran's men went and they brought the guard back with them. He had wrapped a scarf around his head to make it look as though he were sick. He was as white as a dead person.

"What happened to you? Are you ill?" they asked him.

"I swear that today I have seen Azrail (ahz-ray-ihl), the angel of death who will come to take our souls away," he answered.[3] "I can't explain it all to you. Here, I have written everything down."

When Esfesyar read what the guard had seen at Mêrgezer he was furious. "Who has come to my highlands and settled there?" he said. "I want him out of my way so that I don't have to bring about his death." He turned to Piran and said, "What man dares bring his cattle to Mêrgezer and graze them?"

"My advice is to bury this piece of paper under forty feet of earth and forget about the highlands this year," said Piran. "Just pretend that we don't want to go there. I tell you it must be Rustemê Zal and his commanders who have settled there. He has come to take revenge for the death of his son, Zorav. If we go and fight him, he'll kill all of us."

Esfesyar turned to Humanê Veysî (huh-mahn-ay vehy-see). He was his advisor as well as being Piran's brother. "Human, what do you suggest?"

"Forget about this letter from your guard," Human replied. "I suggest that you write your own letter ordering all of your men together and we'll go and fight."

"I like your idea better," Esfesyar said. "Your brother, Piran, always makes me afraid."

"I am at your service," said Human.

Esfesyar collected his soldiers by writing letters to the people that Human suggested, calling on them to come and fight.

Piran had fifteen hundred fighters, Keshê Kabusê (keh-shay kah-buh-say) had seventeen hundred fighters, Bahumanê Behrî (bah-huh-mahn-ay beh-ree) had eighteen hundred fighters, and Qehirê Kur (keh-hih-ray kuhr) had fifteen hundred fighters. They all arrived as guests of Esfesyar. So many soldiers came to Esfesyar's town that there was not enough room for them. Every road and every place was crowded with pelewans. Esfesyar set up tents all around the city for these fighters. He gathered them from March 21, the time of the Newroz festival, until September, and then they made for the Mêrgezer highlands.

The day that Esfesyar left, Rustem slept very well the night before. When he awoke, he saw that his men were still sleeping. Those who were not sleeping had gone hunting, and others were playing games. Rustem called out, "Hey, come together. Come here." They gathered around him and said, "What has happened? Why have you called us together?" Rustem said to them all, "Is this your land? Is this the land of your fathers that you have come here to play and to go hunting? Don't you know that at any moment Esfesyar and his men may attack us and we won't be able to escape?"

Rustem ordered Tûz to go and defend Hîmevanê mountain. Tûz took his fighters and went there. Givû was given the bridge to defend and Mêran was told to defend Kîsebê castle. Then they brought Rustem his grandson who was the son of Zorav. They all wanted Rustem to give him an Aryan name. So Rustem named him Bîrzê pelewan, or Bîrzê the warrior, and ordered him to defend another mountain.

Now that he had commanders defending all four parts of Mêrgezer highlands, Rustem stationed his own men everywhere. Gûrgîn and Zavare he sent up to the summit of Hîmevanê mountain to survey the land and keep watch. Those two went to the peak and made themselves some tea. They took turns standing guard.

It was the afternoon, and it was Zavare's turn to keep watch while Gûrgîn slept. Zavare saw through his spyglass that there were soldiers everywhere. He couldn't even see the end of them there were so many coming their way. He pushed his leg against Gûrgîn to wake him, "Wake up! That rotten Esfesyar has brought an army."

Gûrgîn looked over and saw all the soldiers. He was angry with Zavare. "I wish you weren't related to Rustem. How can you be so afraid?"

"I'm not afraid of anything. How can you say such a thing to me?" Zavare said.

Both of them encouraged each other to be fearless and then they went down to halt the enemy. For three days and three nights, they didn't let a single enemy soldier pass. There was blood and bodies everywhere.

Esfesyar turned to Piran and said, "Our soldiers can't move forward and we have lost so many of them. What's going to happen?" Piran said, "Oh-lo! You didn't listen to me. You listened to my brother Human. Just look through your spyglass and you can see that there are only two weak men defending Hîmevanê, and yet they have killed so many of our soldiers that the corpses are floating in blood. What will happen if we come across their serious fighters?"

Esfesyar looked through his spyglass and he could see that thousands of his soldiers had been killed and they were all floating in blood. He commanded his men to walk forward, and they all marched forward.

Zavare said, "Gûrgîn, they are all coming toward us. I don't think we can resist this huge number. I am of the Zal family and I have sworn that I will never turn my back on a fight. I can't leave. But one of us has to rouse our people so that they won't be ambushed."

"I won't leave," said Gûrgîn. "I'm just as fresh as I was on the first day I entered this battle."

"Well, I'm wounded," said Zavare. "I can't go. You have to be the one to tell them that danger is approaching."

"If I go, then you will say 'Gûrgîn left me alone at the front,' so I won't go. I don't want you to say this behind my back."

"I promise you that such words will never come out of my mouth. I will always praise you and say how heroically you fought."

"Alright, Zavare, then I'll go."

Gûrgîn spurred his horse and went off. He reached the main camp and shouted out, "They have killed Zavare!" Rustem said, "Have they killed him?" "It is sure that they have," Gûrgîn said, "and now Esfesyar's men are headed toward the bridge."

"Well he is a man, and he can be killed. But tell me, did he fight well or not?"

"It is three days that Zavare has been in the battle," said Gûrgîn. "The fight that he fought is unique. Neither you nor your father nor your ancestors have done such great things."

"Yes, I know him and his family," said Rustem. "I know how great he is. That's why I positioned him there."

Rustem alerted all of his soldiers that Esfesyar's men were approaching the bridge. Now up until that time, no pelewan—no warrior—had been able to fight with both a spear and a mace at the same time. But when Givû fought, he fought with weapons in both hands. Givû held the bridge. He was laying waste to Esfesyar's army when suddenly he saw Zavare coming toward him. Givû took Zavare to one side and he fell down unconscious. He gave him some mey to drink, and in half an hour he came around as though he had never been wounded at all.

Esfesyar asked Piran what was happening and Piran said, "Our fighters can't move. We've been stopped here and we cannot go on. Pick up your spyglass and look at the man defending the bridge, then you'll see the real fighters." When Esfesyar saw Givû's skill and his heroic defense of the bridge he said, "I wish you were my fighter, Givû. I wish you were a Turan and you were with me. I would feed you with meat and rice and mey and make you so comfortable in my town." He said to Piran, "Is there a pelewan among us who can fight him? Can someone cut off his head and bring it to me?"

At that moment Piran made a mistake. He said, "I have a younger brother who can defeat him. His name is Qeyhremanê Veys (kehy-hreh-mahn-ay vays)." Now Piran was an Aryan, not a Turan like Esfesyar. Esfesyar became suspicious of Piran and said to him, "You have such a fighter for a brother and you didn't bring him along? It is because of this that there is the saying "Rehdibin bost dijibin nabin dost": "Your beard can grow one handbreadth, but your enemy can never be your friend."

"I am not your enemy," Piran said. "When we left, he was sleeping and we didn't want to wake him up."

Now as they were speaking, Qeyhreman woke and saw that there was no one else in the town. "Where are all the fighters?" he asked. When he was told where they had gone and for what reason, he followed the path that they had taken. While Esfesyar and Piran were talking about him, he suddenly appeared.

"Here he is!" said Piran.

"Bring me Givû's head," Esfesyar said to him. "If you do, you and your family will have the authority to live wherever you want in this country. You will have the freedom to punish or command people to get whatever you want." They encouraged Qeyhreman and Qeyhreman went to fight him.

Givû was not on his horse; he was on the ground. Qeyhreman swung his mace at Givû, hitting him and dragging him two hundred meters, throwing him from the bridge. People shouted to Rustem to come, saying, "They have killed Givû and now soldiers are crossing the bridge!" Rustem got on his horse and rode swiftly over. He grabbed Qeyhreman and threw him on the bridge so hard that he broke his backbone in seven places. Qeyhreman couldn't move again. Esfesyar's soldiers had crossed the bridge, but Rustem fought them back. Rustem called out, asking if Givû had really been killed. He was told that Givû was still alive, that he was unconscious and maybe he would come around. Givû was given some mey to drink, and in half an hour he stood up as if he had never been hit, as if he had never been in the fight. It was as if he were on the first day. He told Rustem to withdraw and he would defend the bridge.

Rustem called his people to come together because he wanted to speak with them. "In such a fight killings are as nothing," he told them. "There are many deaths when the battle is in full swing. Let's open the gates to the plain," he said. "We're here. Let them come in and we'll have a big fight."

"You are the one who knows," they said.

He called all of his commanders to come to the plain. Rustemê Zal and his three lead commanders, Tûz, Givû and Mêran came together and opened the way.

Esfesyar looked at his men and they were an endless line of people. He couldn't even see the end of them as they approached. Esfesyar's men came at Rustemê Zal's men from all four sides at once. But whoever entered the arena was killed. Esfesyar said, "Yes, Piran, you were right. Today is the end of our time. We can't beat them. Let's go back."

Now when Qeyhreman was killed, his brother, Piran, asked Esfesyar to give him fifty commanders so that with them he could go to fight Rustemê Zal. "Take them and go," said Esfesyar. "You are free." And he gave him fifty men with their horses. Piran had a special way to get to the arena. When he went that way, no one could see him. Piran and his men approached Rustemê Zal's tent. One of Rustemê Zal's commanders saw them and said to Piran, "Do you think you can escape from this place?"

Rustem heard this and came out of his tent. He put one of his feet in the stirrup of his horse Reshbelek and galloped away ten or fifteen meters. For the first time in his life, Rustem rode away from his enemy. Piran called out, "Don't look so overjoyed as you ride away. You cannot escape from me!"

"I'm not escaping from you," Rustem replied. "The arena is too small and I'm making more room for war."

The battle began and Rustem killed Piran and his fifty soldiers. What was left of Esfesyar's army was already retreating.

Now Esfesyar had a horse called Sheshalingê Behrî (shehs-ah-lihn-gay beh-ree). It had six legs. As Esfesyar was riding away on his horse, Bîrz, the son of Zorav, and the grandson of both Esfesyar and Rustem, rode in front of Esfesyar's horse. "Are you going to kill me?" Esfesyar asked. "No, I won't kill you. You're my grandfather. But I am going to take your horse to my other grandfather, Rustemê Zal." Bîrz took the six-legged horse to Rustem and they couldn't prevent him from doing this.

Now it was Rustem's tradition that, whenever he won a battle, he would sit on the throne of the one whom he had conquered. Rustem sat on Esfesyar's throne and Esfesyar, as a present and as a sign of defeat, put gold on a plate. A girl presented the gold to Rustemê Zal. Rustem then left Esfesyar's kingdom and went back home. And that is how one small chapter in the life of Rustemê Zal ends.

Notes: Collected in May 2005 from a sixty-year-old man, Sîpan Mountain region, Kurmancî, translated by Çeto Ozel.

1. Throughout this tale, the ending vowel ê of the first name is dropped when the last name is not included. For example, Rustemê Zal is called Rustem, and Humanê Veysî is referred to as Human.

2. When the snow in the highlands has melted enough so that there are streaks of grass, this is called belekevî, a dappled white and green.

3. In Islam it is believed that when someone dies, an angel comes to take the person's soul away. That angel is called Azrail, so, in essence, this man has seen his death.

Humorous Stories

Darên hişk bi avê mezin nabin.

A piece of wood won't grow by watering.

—Kurdish Proverb

Kurdish Storyteller, 2005. Photo by the author.

The Biggest Lie

Uncles often play an important role in the coming of age of their young nephews. As in this story, there can be a great deal of fun and rivalry between them. There are even different titles for each of the uncles, depending on whether they are on the mother's or father's side of the family. The young boy in this tale vies with his uncle for a loaf of bicik, a round bread made with eggs and butter. (Look for the recipe for bicik on page 12). In the story, there is also reference made to the mountain highlands called zozan. These highlands are very important in Kurdish culture. Every summer the herds are moved there, where it is cooler and where there is more water and fresh grass. This story was collected in both Dimilî and English from Cafer Sahin, originally from Dêrsim, in the Kurdish region of Turkey. Cafer used colorful vernacular in his English telling of "The Biggest Lie." I have tried to keep this flavor in my retelling.

A young shepherd boy came home from the mountains one day. He had been tending the sheep since early morning and he was very hungry. He said to his mother, "I'm hungry, mother. Do we have any bread?"

"Oh, my child," his mother replied, "we have no more bread and it will take several hours for the dough to rise. But your uncle is down at the mill grinding flour, and he probably made some of your favorite bread, bicik (bih-jihk). Why don't you go there and maybe you can eat with him?"

So the boy walked down to the watermill. He was very hungry and he walked fast, but it still took him half an hour to get there.

His uncle was sitting outside the mill and he saw his nephew coming fast down the hill. "Oh no," he thought, "it's my nephew and he's always hungry. He'll probably want to eat with me and I only have one little loaf of bicik. But he's only a kid, I'm gonna trick him and I'll get to eat all of the bicik myself."

So the boy arrived. He was very hungry, but he was nice and polite saying, "Hello, Uncle, how've you been? It's been such a long time since I've seen you. I missed you. And Mother told me you probably cooked something to eat, so I came here."

"Well," said his uncle, "your mother was right. I did cook something. But what I made is very little, just one loaf of bicik. Now if both of us eat this bread, neither of us are gonna

be full. So we have a problem. I think only one of us should eat." The nephew looked at him with big eyes.

"How's that gonna work, Uncle? You know I'm a kid—kids should eat."

"No, you're not a kid anymore; you're a big boy. We're two men here. We're gonna play a little game. Whoever wins the game is gonna get the bicik."

"What kind of game, Uncle?"

"Well, we're gonna lie. Whoever tells the biggest lie gets to eat the bicik."

"OK," said the boy. "Go ahead. Start! Start it up!"

The uncle was very sure of himself. He thought, "This kid cannot lie as much as me!" He said, "Last winter I needed firewood, so I went into the woods with my great axe. In the middle of the woods, I found a tree. It was a really big walnut tree. It was so big, it was so wide, I can't even tell you how wide it was. I went up to it with my axe, and I started hitting that tree with my axe and hitting that tree with my axe. For forty days and forty nights I chopped that tree with my axe. And at the end of forty days and forty nights I only reached the middle of that tree. In the middle of that tree was a hollow, and out of it ran a black bear and nine of her babies. So that's how big that tree was."

Well the kid was not impressed.

"That's it?" he said.

"Yeah," said his uncle. "That's it. This is it."

"You want me to go ahead?"

"Yeah," said his uncle, "go ahead."

"OK!" said the kid. "You know, every year Grandmother and I take our herds up to zozan (zoh-zahn), to the cooler places in the mountains. Last year, along with our herds of sheep and goats we brought our bees. From those bees we get the most delicious honey, but it's very hard work."

"Why?" said his uncle.

"Well, we have one hundred hives and one hundred bees in every hive. We have to make sure that none of them gets lost. Every morning we have to open the hive, count the bees as they're going out. And every evening we have to open the hive, count the bees as they're coming in. It's very difficult because sometimes they all come at once and you have to count very, very fast."

"One evening we were counting the bees, and the last bee didn't come at all. We knew this bee. He was a bad little bee; he would never come on time. He would always keep us waiting. But this time Grandmother and I were very worried because this morning, when he left, he had a limp. My grandmother was so upset, she said, 'Oh that poor little bee with the limp, I'm so worried about him. Go, child, go and bring me my darning needle!' I brought the big needle and she looked through the eye of that needle and peered through the eye of that needle. She looked and looked into the distance, 'Wow!' she said. 'Our bee is miles and miles away in Heleb, Syria.[1] Oh no! They've harnessed our bee to a yoke, put a bull beside him, and they're making him plow the earth. They shouldn't do that. He's hurt; he has a limp. We have to go get our bee! Come, child, bring me my chair.' I brought her chair and she sat right down. 'Stand behind me, my child, and hold on tight. We're going to go get our bee!' I stood behind my grandmother and held on tight and suddenly we shot up into the air. We flew through the air and all the way to Heleb."

His uncle can't believe what a crazy story his nephew is making up. He knows he's been beaten already, but he wants to see how far this kid can go—what are the limits of this kid?

"When we landed in Heleb, sure enough, there's our bee dragging the plow behind him. We went up to that ploughman and said, 'Don't you have any shame? Putting our bee on the plow with that bull. You could have hurt your bull. Our bee is much too strong for him. You'd better give us back our bee.' He gave us back our bee and we saw that it had a little splinter in the back of its neck—probably from the wooden yoke. My grandmother said, 'Don't worry, my child, I know how to take care of this. Go find me the green skin of a walnut.' So I brought her the green skin of a walnut and she rubbed it on that little bee's back and she rubbed it on that little bee's back. For forty days and forty nights she rubbed the walnut skin on that little bee's back. And after forty days, wouldn't you know, out of the back of that bee a tree starts growing. It's a walnut tree . . . a really big walnut tree!"

"What!" said the uncle. He knows it's *his* walnut tree in the kid's story.

"That walnut tree grew so big. It grew so wide, I can't even tell you how wide it was. Everyday we had fresh walnuts to eat. But one day, I picked up a rock and threw it up into the branches to get more walnuts. When the rock came down, it turned into a lot of earth so then we had a big field where we could grow tomatoes." By this point, the kid's uncle had had enough.

"That's it, that's it!" he said. "Take the bread and go! You win! You win! Go and take your limping bee with you!"

So you see, that boy was very creative just for a piece of good Kurdish bread.

Notes: Collected in March 2002 from Cafer Sahin, Dêrsim region, Dimilî, and English. This story was collected with the assistance of Yuksel Serindag.

1. Heleb is the Kurdish place name for Aleppo, Syria.

Three Donkeys Like You!

Y *ek hebû û yek tûnebû* . . . Once there was and once there wasn't a family: a mother, a father, a son, and a daughter. One day, visitors came to their home, and although food was already prepared, there was nothing for the guests to drink. So the father sent his daughter down to the river to bring the guests some fresh water.

As the girl was filling her pitcher, she started crying and crying. She sat down by the riverbank sobbing and crying and wailing and she never went back to the house. The husband asked his wife to go and see what had happened. She went in search of her daughter, and what did she find but her daughter crying and sobbing by the riverside.

"Daughter, why are you crying?" she asked.

"Oh Mother, what if I get married to someone who lives in that village on the other side of the river. And if I have a son, and he comes one day to visit you, he might fall into the river and drown and then what will I do?"

The mother started crying, too. They held each other and cried and cried for the boy who might one day be drowned in the river.

Back at the house, everyone was thirsty and waiting for water. "Father," the son asked, "can you go and find out what happened? Mother and sister never came back."

The father went in search of them and what did he find but the two of them sobbing in each other's arms by the riverside.

"Why are you crying?" he asked his wife.

"Oh husband, what if our daughter gets married to someone who lives in that village on the other side of the river? And if she has a son, and her son comes one day to visit us, he might fall into the river and drown and then what will we do?"

The father started crying, too. And they all sat by the riverside sobbing and crying in each other's arms.

At last, the son decided to go and find out what had happened to the rest of his family. He found them all in tears by the riverside.

"What happened?" he asked them. "Why are you all crying?"

"Oh," his parents replied, "what if your sister gets married to someone that lives in that village on the other side of the river? And if she has a son and her son comes one day to visit us, he might fall into the river and drown and then what will we do?" And they all began sobbing and weeping again.

"What are you, donkeys? That's a ridiculous story!" he said. "Now come back to the house so we can take care of our guests."

After the guests were gone, the son said, "I'm going to travel the world to see if I can find three people who are bigger donkeys than you are. If I find them, I'll forgive you. But if not, I'm going to tie the three of you together and toss you into the deepest part of the river."

The boy set off looking for people more foolish than his family. He came across a man running as fast as he could while carrying a heavy chest, called a sandiq, on his back.

"Where are you going in such a hurry?" he called out.

"I have stolen this sandiq," said the man. "And they'll be coming after me, perhaps even on horseback."

"Your sandiq looks too heavy for just one person. Let me carry it awhile for you."

"That would be helpful," said the robber. And the boy jogged along beside him with the sandiq on his back.

"See how well you're running now?" said the youth. "You know, you can get away much faster if you're not carrying this sandiq. Why don't I take it from you so that you can escape faster? If someone shows up asking if I saw a man carrying a sandiq, I'll say 'yes' and send him off in a different direction from the direction you went."

"Thank you so much," said the robber. And he ran away without his stolen goods.

The youth hid the sandiq. A man on horseback came riding up and asked the youth if he had seen anyone going by with a sandiq.

"Yes, I have," said the boy.

"Where has he gone?" asked the man. "And how can I catch him?"

"He went down that path," said the boy, pointing him in the wrong direction. "But he was going very slowly because he was on a horse. He would have travelled faster if he were on foot."

"Why is that?" asked the man.

"Well, as everyone knows, horses have to use all four legs when they travel. A horse takes one step, two steps, three steps, four. That man would have been much faster if he were on foot. Then instead of travelling one step, two steps, three steps, four, he would have been able to run one-two, one-two. It's much faster."

"You're right!" said the man. "You've given me an idea about how to be quicker!" And giving the boy his horse, he ran off on foot, one-two, one-two, to try to catch the man who had stolen his sandiq.

The boy continued on his way, not too short, not too long, looking for the third foolish donkey. He came across a man ploughing his field.

"Good health to you!" said the boy.

"Thank you," said the ploughman.

"You're welcome," said the boy. "You look hot and thirsty. Would you like me to watch the oxen for you while you get a drink of water?"

"Thank you," said the ploughman.

The ploughman went down to the river to get a drink of water. While he was gone, the boy broke the yoke holding the two oxen together. He led one of the oxen away and then came back and put ox dung all over the end of the yoke that had held the first ox.

When the farmer returned, the boy ran up to him crying out that while he had been gone one of his oxen had died and flown up to heaven. "Look," said the boy, "his dung fell down as he was flying up into the sky and it landed all over this yoke." The farmer looked at the manure on the end of the yoke and his eyes grew wide. He sat down and began crying and crying for his poor ox that had flown up to heaven.

The boy went back home with the sandiq, the horse and the ox. He called his father, his mother and his sister together and said, "Thank goodness I found three people more foolish than you! It's true that you are donkeys, but I forgive you because there are much bigger donkeys in this world! Look, from them I got this sandiq, this horse, and this ox."

Now our tale is told. May the listeners' parents lie in peace, but not the holes or ears in the walls![1]

Notes: Collected in 2002 from Hanim Aytac, Xarpût (Elazig) region, Kurmancî, translated by Çeto Ozel.

1. The "holes or ears in the wall" refer to people who might be spying.

Muxtaro

ek hebû û yek tûnebû . . . Once there was and once there wasn't a village. In that village lived a young boy who, on the day he was born, was given the name of Muxtaro (mukh-tah-roh). (Muxtaro means "village chief " or "mayor" in Kurdish.) Muxtaro and his mother were very poor; the boy's father had died, so it was just the two of them trying to survive.

Muxtaro grew up and became a smart young man. But although he knew many things, when he looked for work he found no job, no work, nothing to do. Muxtaro became very worried; they needed food to survive. He thought and thought and finally he came up with a plan.

"Mother," he said, "I have an idea. Can you please give me the cow?"

Muxtaro took their cow away, slaughtered it, and cut its meat into pieces for kebabs. His mother was very upset.

"Muxtaro," she said, "what are you doing? You've killed the cow and now we're not going to have any milk, or cheese, or anything to eat."

"Wait and see what's going to happen," replied her son.

Muxtaro invited everyone in the village to a big feast. Everyone came and ate very well, but when they left, no one even bothered to tell Muxtaro or his mother thank you very much.

"Don't worry, mother," said Muxtaro, "soon all of these people will be inviting us over for a meal."

Days passed, and they weren't invited anywhere for any food at all. They grew hungrier and hungrier. Muxtaro realized things couldn't go on this way, and again he went deep into thought. Finally he said to his mother, "Mother, the people of the village have cheated us. Not one person has invited us for a meal in return for our generosity. It's my fault that we have nothing, so I'm going to try to find another way."

Muxtaro took the skin of their cow and made a sack from it. He blew it full of air until it looked quite full, and then he set off down the road. Along the way, he met a shepherd who had a lot of sheep and cows. The shepherd asked him, "What's that you're carrying?"

"Oh," said Muxtaro, "this is the skin of my cow and inside it is filled with gold."

The shepherd immediately invited Muxtaro to be his guest for dinner and to stay as long as he liked. In the middle of the night, Muxtaro slowly opened up his sack and let the air out. Phhhhhh … Phhhhhh … Phhhhhh … With the air all gone, his sack was flat and empty.

Muxtaro ran out of the house in his nightclothes yelling, "Hello! Help! Help! Help!" The shepherd and his wife came out to see what Muxtaro was yelling about and Muxtaro said to them, "While I was sleeping you took all of my gold! Look, my sack is empty! I'm going to tell the Axa (ah-khah), who rules the region, that you robbed me."

The shepherd became very worried and thought to himself, "The Axa rules over us. If he hears that I've robbed someone of their gold, he's going to kill us." The shepherd decided that to get Muxtaro to be quiet, he would give him a lot of gold and then send him on his way. Muxtaro put the gold into his sack and set off. He used the money well and became very rich. In fact, he became the Axa of the neighboring region. In this new place, he and his mother had a whole flock of sheep and a grand house from which they could see all around.

The people from his old village learned about all of this and they wondered at it. They talked among themselves, saying, "Muxtaro went to another village, and he became very rich. Let's ask him how he became so wealthy." All the people from his old village came to see Muxtaro, and they asked him, "How did you get all of these animals and riches?"

"Everything came from the sea," he said.

"Muxtaro," the people said, "that's impossible. How can you get all of these things from the sea?"

"I'll show you," said Muxtaro. "There's a lot of gold in the sea if you know where to look for it."

"Well, what about these animals? Where did they come from?" they asked him.

"I harvested these animals from the sea as well," he said.

The people didn't believe him, but Muxtaro promised to show them the very next day.

Muxtaro was very angry with the people from his old village. The next day, before he took them to the water, he placed a tall shepherd's crook as far as he could out into the ocean. Then he invited everyone down to the water's edge.

The people looked out to sea and said, "We don't see anything. How did you get animals and gold from the sea?"

"Look," said Muxtaro, "someone is out there gathering sheep right now! Go see what animals you can harvest." The people saw the shepherd's crook out in the water and thought that there was a shepherd under the water gathering up the animals. Everybody jumped into the water and set out in that direction. One said, "Help!" and one said, "There's nothing!" An old woman stood on the shore and told her son, "Jump further, maybe you can bring back a water buffalo! Jump further. Go! Go!"

The people went out further and further, but at the same time, the tide was coming in. In the end, both the shepherds crook and the people were all washed away. Muxtaro brought his mother back to their grand house, and there they lived in wealth until they died very rich, very well, and very happy. And that is the story of Muxtaro.

Note: Collected in May 2005, from a twenty-six-year-old man, Mûş region, Kurmancî.

The Lord of Luck

*T*here once lived a cowherd who was very unhappy with his lot. Every day he looked after the villagers' cows, but he never seemed to have much to show for it no matter how hard he worked.

One day while he was watching the cows, he saw a rich man walking toward the lake. At the same time, a horse emerged from the lake covered with gold and jewels. The rich man took its halter and began leading it away.

"What's your secret?" asked the cowherd. "I pasture the cows here everyday, I water them at the lake, but I never have any good fortune like this. Can you tell me why I'm not successful like you?"

"Yes, I can," said the man. "Your problem is that the lord of your luck is asleep. You only have to wake him up. After you do that, then you will have riches too."

The cowherd went home and immediately announced to everyone that from now on they would have to look after their own cows. He was leaving the village in search of the lord of his luck and when he found him, he would return a rich man. He said good-bye and set off on his way.

As he passed through the mountains he came across a bear. The bear asked him where he was going and he told the bear his story. The bear listened and then said, "When you find the lord of your luck, will you ask a question for me?"

"Certainly," said the man.

"Ask him why I'm so ill. I never get any better. What must I to do to get better again?"

"I'll ask," said the cowherd, and he continued on his way.

In his travels he came across a farmer. The farmer also asked him where he was going. After he told his story, the farmer said, "When you find the lord of your luck can you ask what the problem is with my land? There's a certain part of my field that won't grow any wheat at all. Please ask why this is so."

The cowherd traveled on and on. He journeyed so far that he reached a different kingdom. After he stayed there a while, news reached the Sultan that there was a stranger in the land. The Sultan summoned the cowherd to him and asked him to explain his presence.

The cowherd told of his journey to awaken the lord of his luck, and the Sultan said, "When you find him can you ask a question for me? Ask why I never win a battle against the neighboring kingdom. No matter how many soldiers I use or how hard or well we fight, we never win, we only lose."

"I will ask," said the man and he continued on his way.

At last he came to a sea so wide, he didn't know how he would ever cross it. As he stood thinking about this problem, a big fish swam near.

"Why are you standing there and looking toward the other shore?" asked the fish.

"I know that the lord of my luck must be over there," said the man, "but I don't know how to cross."

"I'll help you to cross," said the fish, "if you'll ask a question for me. Ask why I have such a terrible pain in my head. It never leaves me night or day."

"I will ask," said the man. And the fish brought him to the other shore.

At last the cowherd found the land of luck. The lords of everyone else's luck were very busy working and doing things but his was sleeping just as had been foretold to him.

He shook the lord of his luck awake and chastised him saying, "Because of you I'm always poor and never have any good fortune. From now on I need you to work hard for me."

The lord of his luck agreed. Then the cowherd asked the lord of his luck to tell him how to solve the problems of the bear, the farmer, the sultan and the fish.

When the cowherd reached the ocean, the big fish was waiting to take him back across. After it had brought him to the opposite shore it said to him,

"Did you ask the lord of your luck why I have such bad headaches?"

"Yes, I did, and he said that you have headaches because there are two great jewels stuck in your head. If you can get someone to kick you in the head, those jewels will come out and you will recover."

"Well," said the fish, "you're right here. Why don't you help me?" The cowherd kicked the fish in the head and, sure enough, two great jewels came out.

"I live in the sea, and I have no use for these," said the fish. "Why don't you take them?"

"No, I will not," said the cowherd. "The lord of my luck is working for me now and all my riches will follow me," and he went on his way.

He arrived at the kingdom of the Sultan and was immediately taken into the throne room where the Sultan was waiting for him.

"Did you learn why I cannot defeat the neighboring kingdom?"

"Yes," said the cowherd. "The reason is that you are a woman; you are not a man. The lord of my luck told me that if you take a lover, even if it is in secret, you will be able to win all of your battles."

"Come," she said, taking off her turban and letting her long hair tumble down. "You can be my lover and all of the kingdoms that I conquer I will give to you."

"Thank you very much," said the cowherd, "but I must be on my way. The lord of my luck is working for me now and all my riches will follow me."

He traveled until he came upon the farmer who had trouble in his field.

"And did the lord of your luck solve the riddle of why no crops will grow in this spot?" he asked.

"He did," said the cowherd. "I was told that there is a treasure buried under that part of the field and because of that nothing will grow."

They both dug into the earth and, sure enough, they unearthed a great treasure chest filled with gold and jewels.

"This is too much for me," said the farmer. "Let me share it with you."

"No," said the man, "the lord of my luck is watching out for me now and all my riches will follow me."

At last he came upon the sick bear high up in the mountains. That evening he told the bear about everything that had befallen him. Of the fish with the jewels in its head, the Sultan who offered him all the kingdoms she conquered and the farmer who wanted to share his treasure with him.

"Of course I refused all that I was offered because the lord of my luck is working for me now and all of my riches will follow me," said the man.

"The lord of your luck solved all these riddles, but did he tell you what I need to do to be healthy again?" asked the bear. "Oh yes," said the man. "He told me that all you need to do is to find the biggest fool in the world, kill him and smear his blood on your chest. Then you'll be cured."

"Excellent," said the bear, "I have certainly found him!"

The bear did as the cowherd had suggested and after that, the bear was cured and lived a long and healthy life.

Note: Collected in May 2005 from a forty-four-year-old man, Erdîş (Erciş/Van) region, Kurmancî.

The Sheep That Strays from the Flock Becomes the Wolf's Dinner

The mountains of Kurdistan provide easy cover for marauding bands of brigands and robbers. Because of this, people would often travel in groups or in a caravan for protection. In Kurdistan there are many stories and songs about traveling in a caravan. Here is one of them.

*I*n a small mountain village, the flour in one of the households had come to an end. So the housewife put some wheat into a sack, her husband loaded it onto his donkey, and he set off to the mill to have it ground into flour.

As he was leaving, his neighbors told him not to go. They told him to wait and travel to the mill together with them in a caravan. But he didn't listen and went off by himself, leading his donkey down the road.

When at last he arrived at the mill there was no one else there, so the miller began grinding his wheat at once. By the time the caravan from his village arrived, his wheat had already been ground into flour and the men in charge of the mill were loading it onto his don-

Kurdish carrying sack—Iraqi Kurdistan circa 1955. Photo courtesy of Rudman Ham.

key. His neighbors again cautioned him against traveling alone. "It's a long way," they said, "and there are many bad things that can happen along the road. Wait and we'll all go together." Even the chief of the caravan told him not to go, but he didn't agree. "I can't wait for you," said the man. "It will be a long time before your wheat is ground and I'm going to set off now."

He took the reins of his donkey and led it away. Little did he know that there were three robbers lying in wait for him farther up the road. When they saw the man with the donkey approaching, the robbers spoke among themselves.

One of the thieves said, "I can steal both the donkey and its burden without the owner even knowing it."

The other thief said, "I can take the donkey and its load to the bazaar and sell them."

The last robber said, "I will steal that man's clothes and leave him naked on the road." After the robbers planned what to do, two of them hid while the other one went farther up the road to where there was a large well.

The owner of the donkey trudged along the road, head down, toward the robbers, slowly leading his donkey along. As he walked past the place where the robbers were hidden, the first thief crept up beside the donkey, slipped the halter off it, and put it over his own face. He then continued to follow the man, trudging along in the same way the donkey had, while his fellow robber came and led the donkey away.

The owner continued to walk for awhile. Once he looked back and, instead of his donkey, at the other end of the reins was a man with a halter over his head. "Brother, in fact, I don't know what to say!" said the owner of the donkey. "The only thing I know is that my loaded donkey was following me. But now I look and, instead of him, you are here. I don't understand how a man can be a donkey."

The robber replied, "Friend, don't be astonished. There is no doubt that sometimes, like a donkey, you cannot think properly, and I think you will understand this some day. Just know that I am that same donkey that was tied in front of your house for years. When I was very small, I was stubborn and mean and, because of that, my mother and my father cursed me. The God of the world accepted their curse and turned me into a donkey.[1] It was only recently that my father and my mother took back their curse and I became a man once more."

"Brother, if that is the situation, take the reins off your neck. Go and meet your father and mother. But before you go, I would like to say something to you. For years you have worked for us. We owe a lot to you and I would like you not to hold anything against us. Please forgive us for the years you have spent in our service."

"Brother, I forgive you, and I also want you not to hold anything against me for leaving you after all these years."

The man also forgave him and they parted.

The third robber saw that the owner of the donkey was coming toward him. He went over to the well and looked at it with a sad expression on his face. The owner of the donkey came over, greeted the thief, and said, "Brother, why are you looking at the well in that way? What has happened that is making you so sad?"

The robber said, "Brother, you don't know what has happened to me. One year ago, I left my house and went away to work, to earn some money and support my family. On the way back home, I arrived at this well intending to rest and also to have a drink of water. But as I bent over the well, my wallet dropped in. I'm afraid of water and I can't go down after it, so I am helpless here."

"Don't worry, brother," the man replied, "it's so easy for me. I myself will dive into the well and retrieve your money."

The man took off his clothes and dove into the water. He dove once and then a second time. But while the poor man was underwater, the robber took all of his clothes and ran off to meet his friends.

The man looked and looked for the wallet in the well, but he couldn't find anything. When he got out, he saw that both the robber and his clothes were gone. He stood by the well naked and desperate. After a while, he saw the caravan coming toward him. What could he do? Everyone saw him without any clothes on, trying to hide behind the well.

The leader of the caravan asked him what had happened, and he told them the whole story. The leader then said, "It is believed that 'if you don't listen to your elders, your ears will turn into the horns of a goat.' It is also said that 'the sheep that strays from the flock becomes the wolf's dinner'. These sayings are not said for nothing, and now you prove that they are true. We told you to wait and go with us, but you didn't listen."

The chief of the caravan walked among the caravan and collected some clothes. The man put on the collected clothes and returned home, empty-handed. When his wife saw him in different clothes and without the donkey and the flour, she wanted to know what had happened. The man told the whole story to his wife and his wife said, "There is a saying and it is not said for nothing, 'A piece of wood won't grow by watering.'[2] This proverb has been said just for you. You are exactly the same foolish person you were when you left. If you travel, you should at least get some new ideas. Now put on your own clothes, go to the bazaar, and buy us another donkey."

The man did as his wife asked. He walked round and round the bazaar until at last he saw his old donkey, with a new halter around its head. One of the thieves was holding the reins, while two men bargained with him over the price. The man rushed over to his old donkey and whispered into its ear, "So, up to your old tricks! What did you do to your parents to make them wish you were a donkey this time? Don't think I will buy you again! If you were mean to your parents you deserve whatever master you may find." He turned to the men bargaining over the donkey and said, "If I were you, I wouldn't buy this donkey."

"Why, what's wrong with this donkey?" the men said. "We can't find anything wrong with it. Why do you say this?"

"All I will tell you is that I had this donkey once, and then I could neither load it nor ride it. It was mine but it wasn't mine."

"Wouldn't it let you load it?" asked one of the buyers.

"No, can you load a human? The donkey you are buying is not really a donkey, it's a man. His mother and father cursed him, so sometimes he's a man and sometimes he becomes a donkey."

As the two buyers watched in amazement the foolish man then spent his good money on a different donkey. Perhaps his wife was right, "A piece of wood won't grow by watering."

Notes: Collected by Abbas Alkan and published in his book *Çîroka Rovî û Gur* [*Stories of Fox and Wolf*], published in 2003 by Weşanên Elma, Istanbul, Turkey, Kurmancî. Translated by Çeto Ozel.

1. It is believed that if your parents curse you and pray to God, God will turn you into whatever animal they wish, a frog or a cat or even a donkey.

2. This saying means that no matter how much attention or advice someone is given, if that person cannot listen or think, he or she can never change.

Teaching Tales

Du henek bi rastekê ne.

Two jokes will make a truth.

—Kurdish Proverb

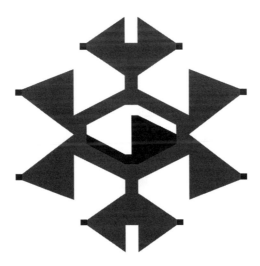

Threshing wheat circa 1955, Iraqi Kurdistan. Photo courtesy of Rudman Ham.

Because of Kurdistan's steep mountains and extreme changes of temperature, a family must work hard to survive, with every member doing his or her share. Hard work is not frowned upon. As in the following story, it is seen as a way to appreciate all that life has to offer.

The Meaning of Life

*O*nce there lived a Padishah, famous for his riches, his palace, and his gardens. He should have been happy, but he didn't enjoy anything that he had. He was not at peace walking in his fine gardens, no food was sumptuous or tasty enough to please him, sleep did not come easily, and when it did it was neither restful nor deep. Truly the Padishah did not understand what made life worth living; he was restless and unhappy.

He began to criticize his people, saying that he didn't understand their ways. "My people sleep too much," he would say, "and they are happy with even a piece of bread and fresh water. I often hear them say that life is good, but what is good about their lives? Why are they so foolish?" The Padishah decided to disguise himself as a common person to see what their life was all about. In this disguise he traveled far, at last arriving at a mountain village where he asked what he could do for work. All that day he helped the man who plowed the fields, keeping the oxen in check, encouraging and guiding them. Sometimes they even plowed on steep ground struggling to keep the furrows straight. They finished work as the sun set.

The evening meal was simple, but never had the Padishah enjoyed food so much. They ate together, seated on the floor, and he felt close to his people and not so alone. That night when he closed his eyes, sleep came deep and restful, and he woke up refreshed. The breakfast of fresh eggs and bread, cheese, jam, and strong tea tasted wonderful. With that and with the clear mountain air he felt glad to be alive. The Padishah then understood the secret of his people. Work was not a burden. Only through difficulty could one relish the times of ease. He returned to his castle with a new understanding of his people and himself.

Note: Collected in 2006 from a thirty-four-year-old woman, Xarpût (Elazig) region, Kurmancî.

The Eyes of a Cat

*O*ne day, the cats decided to change their ways, to stop torturing mice and oppressing them. They announced that they would now travel in the path of religion, tolerance, and peace. When the mice heard about this they were very happy, but they were still suspicious. "We will wait and see what happens," they said. "We have been waiting for this for centuries."

The cats sent a representative to the mice.

"We cats are tired of chasing you around and around," the representative said. "We would like to sign a peace agreement with you."

"Yes, we would like this too," responded the mice. "We are tired of escaping just as you are tired of chasing."

"Well then, let there be peace. You can prove that you trust us by closing up all of the holes and tunnels that you use to escape. As for us, to prove that we have changed our ways, we are going on a pilgrimage to Mecca. On our return you will see that we will never attack you."

So the cats went to the holy land. While they were there, they prayed and swore never to eat mice again. They did all the things they had to do to get away from their sinful ways. After they finished their prayers, they wrapped their heads with colorful scarves to show that they had become pilgrims. Then they lined up and came back home.

Of course on their return, everyone went to visit them and welcome them. They were important now because whoever travels to Mecca is considered to be holy as well. Everyone who went to see them gave them a good report.

The mice heard the news that the cats had returned. But the mice didn't want to listen to rumors that the cats had changed their ways, they wanted to see it with their own eyes. The leaders of the mice held a meeting, and they assigned a delegation of mice to go and see the situation for themselves. Those mice went, and they witnessed the cats sitting quietly with peaceful demeanor. They were all wearing prayer shawls, and they each had a string of prayer beads in their paws. They seemed very changed. The cats welcomed the mice warmly and spoke sweetly to them, showing them their hospitality. The delegation of mice returned home to give their report to their friends.

The mice at home were very excited to hear what had changed. The delegation said, "The cats have really changed. They're sitting peacefully, wearing prayer shawls, and they are all very religious now. They welcomed us and made us feel at home. There is only one problem." "What's that?" asked the other mice. "It's this," said the mice who went to investigate, "Their eyes still watch us in the same way as before."[1]

Notes: Collected in February 2006 from Çeto Ozel, Colemêrg (Hakkari) region, Kurmancî and English.

1. When troublemakers or brutal states don't act peacefully as they have promised, a saying from this story is used to describe them: "Their eyes are the same as before."—"Cawên wan yên berê ne,"—meaning that their violent ways and games have not really changed.

The Serpent and the Man

A shepherd walks among his flock, 2006. Photo courtesy of the author.

The shepherd's crook, or gopal, is associated with mountain people, shepherds, and travelers. It supports them as they walk long distances and long hours at a time and is used to kill poisonous snakes. The crook can be used to pull sheep or goats out of a flock. The gopal is typically waist high and made from the wood of strong trees that do not break easily, such as cherry (kinêr) or ash (benav).

A man was passing along the road one day when he saw a strange thing. A poplar tree had caught fire and, even though it was still green, it was burning from the bottom of the tree upward. At the top of the tree, a serpent, trapped by the fire was calling out, "Traveler, help! Save me from the fire!"

The man felt compassion for the snake. He raised his shepherd's crook up to where the snake was perched. The snake slid onto the crook and wrapped itself around it. Slowly the man lowered it down. But, as he brought the snake down toward his head and neck, the snake sprang onto him wrapping itself tightly around his neck. The serpent was choking him, pulling its coils tighter and tighter so that he couldn't breathe. He knew he was going to die, and he pleaded with the snake.

"Why are you doing this? Don't choke me to death. I helped you."

"Human's are deceitful and untrustworthy," the snake replied. "I will choke you."

"How do you know I can't be trusted?" asked the man.

"I know," said the snake.

"It's not true, and if you like I will call witnesses."

"No, I have the witnesses," the snake said. "Let's go find them."

And they went down the road wrapped tightly together.

On the way they saw a horse standing by the side of the road. The horse's head was hanging down, and it was very weak. The snake spoke to the horse saying, "We have a dispute here and we would like you to be our judge. Tell me, are human's trustworthy or untrustworthy?"

"Untrustworthy," the horse replied.

"Why do you say that?" asked the man.

"When I was young, I was very powerful. I carried humans, and they rode everywhere on my back. But now that I am old, they don't take care of me at all. That is why you see me weak and abandoned by the side of the road."

"That is the first witness," said the snake.

They traveled on together and saw a water buffalo standing in a field.

"Tell me the truth," said the snake. "Are humans trustworthy or untrustworthy?"

"Untrustworthy," said the water buffalo. "Once I was fat and very strong. I gave buckets of milk every day. In those days the humans fed me grass in the summer and hay in the winter, but now that I am older, they have left me here in this field to fend for myself."

"That is the second witness," said the serpent. "When I find the third witness, I will choke you to death!"

They traveled on together and at last they came across a fox.

"Uncle Fox," said the snake, "this man rescued me from a fire, but I still want to strangle him. Answer me a question that will decide his fate: Do you think humans are trustworthy or untrustworthy?"

The fox looked at the snake so close to choking the breath out of this human. He felt sorry for the man and decided he would use his cunning to free him.

"Before I answer that question," said Uncle Fox, "can you tell me who you are?"

"You can see I am the leader," said the snake. "I am deciding the fate of this man. If you agree with me, as the horse and the water buffalo did, that humans are untrustworthy, then I will choke him to death."

"No," said the fox, "you are not the leader! You are a liar and all that you have said is a lie. If you were the leader of this man, you would be out in front of him. Unwrap yourself and come down in the front. Brave leaders are the first to meet any danger."

The snake unwrapped itself and slithered down to the earth in front of the man. The fox cried out, "Stupid, silly man! Take your shepherd's crook and kill it."

The man struck the snake with his gopal and killed it.

"You foolish man," said the fox, "why did you rescue this snake? It cannot help its nature. It's a serpent and it will always try to kill you. Of course all animals know that humans cannot be trusted. Never would you have found a witness to take your side. But, even though I knew that, I saved you. All I ask is that you don't tell the hunters where I am."

The man walked for a while until he saw a group of hunters coming toward him with their dogs and their guns.

"Have you seen any animals?" they asked him.

"Yes," said the man, "there's a fox over there in that direction."

The hunters and their dogs went after the fox. The fox dodged all of the hunters and confused them. He was so cunning that he saved himself. After he had escaped from the last of the dogs, he made his way back and placed himself right in front of the man.

"You betrayed me," the fox said. "If I had said the same as the other two witnesses, the snake would have killed you. But I was sad for you and so I tried to make you safe. We animals are the ones who are trustworthy. I could easily play a game with you right now, but I won't. You, however, are not faithful; you always betray us. Really, the human is not to be trusted."

Note: Collected in May 2005 from eighty-one-year-old man, Kurmancî, Wan (Van) region.

The Shepherd Who Told
Too Many Lies

This story told by shepherds in the Ararat region, may have a common source with the Aesop's fable "The Boy Who Cried Wolf."

*I*n a small village there lived a shepherd whose job was to take care of the sheep from many households. Every day, he would take the flock up into the mountains along with a young shepherd boy who was there to help him. One day, he was bored and he got an idea for some excitement. He told the shepherd boy to run down to the village and tell everyone to come at once because the wolves were attacking the sheep. "Alright, Apo (ah-poh)," the boy said, using the Kurdish word for "uncle," a term of respect and endearment for an older man, "I will do it." The shepherd boy didn't think about whether he was doing right or wrong.

When the villagers heard the news, they grabbed their guns and jumped onto their horses, arriving there as quickly as they could. But when they got there, they didn't see any wolves at all—only the shepherd sitting on a rock and laughing at them. "Ha, ha, ha, ha! Ha, ha, ha, ha, ha! Ha, ha, ha!" He laughed and laughed at them.

The shepherd liked the joke he played on the people, and he did the same thing again and again. Each time he would send the boy to the village saying that the wolves were attacking the sheep, and each time the villagers raced to their aid only to find the shepherd laughing at their distress.

The year passed, it was a wintry day and everywhere there was snow. The people in the village didn't have any dried grass left to give to their animals because there had been a drought the summer before. They told the shepherd to bring the sheep to the mountains to find some places not covered by the snow where there might be grass.

Now in winter, there is not much of anything at all for the animals to eat, no matter if they are tame or wild. So in wintertime, the wolves are ravenous because the smaller animals are in hiding and the domestic animals are kept in the village. When the shepherd and his young assistant brought the sheep to the mountain, a group of twenty or more wolves started circling their animals and began to attack the sheep. The shepherd said to the young boy, "Run to the village! Tell them that a big group of wolves is attacking us. Tell them we

---

need help right away or soon these wolves will kill all of our animals." He sent the boy down to the village just as before, except this time it was really happening.

The boy ran to the village telling everyone, "Hurry! A big pack of wolves is attacking our sheep right now!" He tried to convince them that it was really happening, but not one person believed him. He returned to the flock knowing that it might already be too late and when he arrived most of the sheep had been killed. "Apo," he said to the shepherd, "I told them, but nobody believed me. They all think we're joking again."

Unfortunately, this time it was a true story, and the two were responsible for the loss of many animals because of all the silly jokes they had played in the past.

The message of this story is: Don't lie. If people think you are a liar, they will never believe what you say. They won't help you because they won't know whether you are telling the truth or not.

Note: Collected in January 2002 from Mehmet Akbas, Bazîd (Doğubayazit), Mount Ararat Region, Kurmancî and English.

Wolf at the Door

*Y*ek hebû û yek tûnebû . . . Once there was and once there wasn't a story about a wolf and a family of sheep. Every summer, when the weather became hot, the shepherd would take his sheep to the rich pasturelands high up in the mountains, the high-lands called zozan (zoh-zahn). One year, one of the ewes had newborn lambs that were too young to travel, so they all stayed behind. The ewe named one of her lambs Shengay and the other Pengay.

As summer went on, the good grass in the lowlands was all gone and the mother had to travel higher up for better food. She said to her babies,

> *"My Shengay, my Pengay!*
> *The grass on the lowlands is done,*
> *So up to zozan I run,*
> *Till back from grazing I come,*
> *Please open the door to no one."*

The mother traveled far for food. When she returned, she stood outside the door and said,

> *"My Shengay, my Pengay!*
> *My journey to zozan is done,*
> *I grazed on the grasses each one,*
> *The milk to my udders has come,*
> *Please open the door to your mom."*

As the mother was saying these words, a wolf was listening near the door. He saw that when the two little lambs heard their mother's voice, they happily opened the door. The next day, their mother left for zozan again and the wolf approached the door saying,

> *"My Shengay, my Pengay!*
> *My journey to zozan is done,*
> *I grazed on the grasses each one,*
> *The milk to my udders has come,*
> *Now open the door to your mom."*

The babies said, "No! You don't sound like our mother. We won't open the door."

"What does your mother's voice sound like?" asked the wolf.

Shengay and Pengay said, "Our mother's voice is clear and her legs are white. Your voice is rough and your legs are dark. You are a wolf and you will come and eat us."

The wolf hid himself nearby until the mother came back. The mother came to the door and said,

"My Shengay, my Pengay!
My journey to zozan is done,
I grazed on the grasses each one,
The milk to my udders has come,
Please open the door to your mom."

Shengay and Pengay opened the door. Both of them went to their mother and happily drank the milk. But the wolf outside the door had listened to how sweetly the ewe had spoken to her children, and he had seen how white her legs were. The next day, when the lambs' mother went to zozan again, the wolf covered his legs with flour, and clearing and sweetening his voice with honey, he called from outside the door,

"My Shengay, my Pengay!
My journey to zozan is done,
I grazed on the grasses each one,
The milk to my udders has come,
Now open the door to your mom."

The lambs heard a sweet voice and saw legs that looked white so they opened the door. When they opened the door, the bloodthirsty wolf rushed in and gobbled up Shengay. But Pengay hid herself and the wolf didn't find her.

When the mother returned she saw that the door was open. She went inside and there was the wolf sleeping on his back with his belly full and swollen. Little Pengay came out and told his mother what had happened to Shengay. The wolf was sleeping soundly, so while he slept they both dragged him down to the lake. There they cut his belly open, and little Shengay popped out as good as new. They filled the wolf's stomach with heavy stones and sewed it back up. The wolf woke up and stumbled over to the lake to get some water. He leaned over to drink and then he fell in and drowned from the weight of the stones. He never bothered Little Shengay or Little Pengay again.

If my story came out right,
Now's the time to say goodnight.

Note: Collected in May 2006 from a forty-six-year-old woman, Mardin region, Kurmancî, translated by Çeto Ozel.

No Sweet Milk, No Gold

Yek hebû û yek tûnebû . . . Once there was and once there wasn't a shepherd. Every day he took his sheep to the mountains to graze. One day, while his flock was grazing, he became thirsty. He took out his shepherd's bowl and milked a ewe and filled his bowl.[1] He saw that his flock had wandered far away, so he set down his bowl on a stone and went to gather his flock and bring them back. When he returned, he saw a snake wriggling over to his bowl of milk to drink.

The shepherd watched the snake; he didn't strike it with his shepherd's crook. He thought, "It's a cute snake." He didn't want to kill it. The shepherd let the snake finish all of the milk. When the snake arrived at the entrance to its hole, it left a piece of gold for the shepherd. It happened this way every day.

Years came and years went; the shepherd became very, very rich. People around him asked him, "Why do you take your sheep to the mountains every day? You're rich. You don't have to do that."

"Well," said the shepherd, "I take the sheep to the mountains because I like to do it."

Years passed; the shepherd grew older and his eldest son was now almost thirty years old. The shepherd said to his son, "I want you to take the flock up into the mountains today. Milk a ewe and place the milk in a bowl. Wait and a snake will come—don't kill it. It will leave you a piece of gold. Never, never do any harm to this snake—never strike it, never touch it. This snake is the secret of our riches." He told his son where to find the snake.

His son went into the mountains to the same place his father always went. He milked the ewe into a bowl and saw the snake come and drink it. The snake left the son a piece of gold and he came back home. The next day, he said to himself, "What a stupid father! Why doesn't he kill the snake and take all of its gold? Well, I'm not going to wait every day. I'm going to get all the gold at once." The next day, while the snake was drinking the milk, the son threw a huge stone at it to crush it. But his aim was bad, and he only cut off the end of the snake's tail. The snake escaped, but the end of its tail was gone.

As the young man was walking away, the snake came up behind him. It attacked him from behind. It sprang at him, entering his body through the back and coming out in the front right where his heart was. The snake killed the young man.

Some time passed; the son did not come home. In the evening the sheep came back by themselves. People in the village gathered around. They asked the shepherd, "Where is your son? Do you know?"

"I don't," the father said, "but it may be that my son is dead."

The father went back to the entrance to the snake's hole, and he saw his son's body there. He also saw the boulder with the piece of the snake's tail near it. He took the body of his son home and buried him in the graveyard.

Two weeks later the father went back to the snake's hole and said, "Brother snake, come out. I still want to be your brother. I can forgive you and forget my son, because I know that it was his fault. I can see that he tried to kill you."

The snake said, "If I come out, even if we are still brothers, when you see me, you will remember the death of your son and you will feel anger toward me. And when I see you, I will remember the hand that caused me to lose my tail. So let us be honest. It's not going to be like we are brothers. Something will stay in our hearts and in our minds. Let's accept that what has happened, happened. After all, it isn't necessary for me to have sweet milk or for you to have gold."

"You are right," said the man, and he returned to his village empty-handed.

Notes: Collected in May 2005 from a fifty-six-year-old shepherd, Kurmancî, Agirî (Ararat) region.

1. When the shepherds go to the mountains, they take a bowl with them so that when they are thirsty or hungry they can milk a ewe, put the milk in a bowl, heat it, and drink it instead of tea.

Credits and Acknowledgments

"The Goranî, Story of Rawchî," © 2006, collected and translated by Mustafa Dehqan [unpublished] retold with permission.

Kurdish proverbs provided by Zerî Înanç used with permission.

Photos from Iraqi Kurdistan, 1954–1956 by Rudman Ham. These photos are appearing in print for the first time.

Rebekah Murphy created the following graphic elements for this book: the map "Kurdistan in the context of the Middle East"; the illustrations in the following chapters: "Recipes," "Games," "Legendary and Heroic Figures," and "Tales of Wonder." In addition, all black and white borders and motifs in the book were abstracted from Kurdish tribal rugs by Rebekah Murphy.

"Rovî û Legleg," "Rovî Bû Zembîl Firoş," and "Pezê Ji Kêrî Biqete Nesîbê Gura Ye" collected by Abbas Alkan and published in *Çîroka Rovî û Gur*, © 2003, translated and retold with permission.

"Sultan Mahmud and Heyas," in "Winter Tales: A Collection of Kurdish Folktales," ©1996, by Leeya Thompson [unpublished] retold with permission.

"The Zay Tree and the Tay Falcon," *International Journal of Kurdish Studies* 13(2): 73–82. Reprinted with permission of The Kurdish Library. Copyright © 1999.

Appendix

Pronunciation Guide—
Kurdish Alphabet

a: (ah) as in father
b: (b) as in boy
c: (j) as in jar
ç: (ch) as in cheerful
d: (d) as in dog
e: (a) short a sound as in at
ê: (ay) long a sound as in hay but without the diphthong; closer to the é sound in French
f: (f) as in far
g: (g) as in gate
h: (h) as in house
i: (ih) short i sound as in it
î: (ee) long e sound as in seen
j: (zh) as in decision; similar to French "j" sound as in "jour"
k: (k) as in kite
l: (l) as in last
m: (m) as in more
n: (n) as in nice
o: (oh) as in own
p: (p) as in pear
q: no English equivalent—a light glottal stop in the throat
r: (r) as in river
s: (s) as in sun
ş: (sh) as in shower
t: (t) as in top
u: (uh) as in put
û: (oo) as in soon
v (v) as in valiant
w (w) as in water
x: (kw) there is no English equivalent; this can be compared with the aspirated Scottish ch sound as in loch
y: (y) as in yearn
z: (z) as in zebra

Index

About the Author and Contributors

Diane Edgecomb, Author and Storyteller

An award-winning storyteller who has created more than twenty performances for adult and family audiences, Edgecomb has been hailed by *Publishers Weekly* as "A storyteller in the grand tradition . . . a virtuoso of the spoken word." She is also the author of several original stories and adaptations of classic myths and legends ranging from children's stories teaching environmental awareness to myths that center around nature and seasonal change. After becoming aware of the regional policies that were undermining the Kurdish storytelling heritage, Edgecomb began documenting these disappearing treasures. In 1999, she began collecting stories from Kurdish refugees in the United States. In 2001, she initiated The Kurdish Story Collection Project, an international endeavor to document and preserve the stories and storytelling traditions of the Kurdish people. With funds from the Sparkplug Foundation, the Ella Lyman Cabot

Fund, and the National Storytelling Network, she made numerous trips to villages in the Kurdish region of Turkey. While there, she succeeded in filming and archiving a large complement of tellers. The selections for this book were made from her collection of more than 150 Kurdish tales and legends. In addition to her writing, Edgecomb has continued her work as a storyteller and experimental theater artist, performing at theaters, museums, colleges, schools, and libraries throughout the United States and abroad. Her audio recordings have received numerous awards and commendations and can be found at www.livingmyth.com.

Mohammed M. A. Ahmed

Dr. Ahmed holds a Ph.D. and M.A. in agricultural economics from Oklahoma State University and has lectured and undertaken socioeconomic development research at the University of Baghdad, Iraq. Dr. Ahmed joined the United Nations as an Economic and Social Affairs Officer in 1969. He first served with the United Nations Food and Agricultural Organization, as resident expert, in Jordan, Rome, Syria, Bahrain, and Sri Lanka and then with the United Nations Economic and Social Commission for West Asia in Beirut, Lebanon. He moved to the United Nations headquarters in New York in 1980, where he served in various capacities. The last post he held at the UN involved helping member states in the articulation and implementation of economic and social development programs at the macro and grassroots levels. After retiring from the UN, he founded the Ahmed Foundation for Kurdish Studies, a nonprofit and nonpartisan organization. Dr. Ahmed has organized four conferences on Kurdish topics and published, in cooperation with Professor Michael Gunter, their outcomes in the following books: *The Kurdish Question and International Law*; *Kurdish Exodus: From Internal Displacement to Diaspora; The Kurdish Question and the 2003 Iraqi War;* and *The Evolution of Kurdish Nationalism.*

Çeto Ozel

Ozel has been indispensable as advisor, translator and contributor to *A Fire in my Heart: Kurdish Tales.* A native Kurmancî speaker from the small mountainous Kurdish town of Shemzinan, near Colemêrg, Ozel is also an English teacher and linguist. He is the author of several books and articles devoted to the Kurdish language. From *Kurdiya Nûjen,* a primer for beginners and elementary students in the Kurdish Kurmancî dialect, to *Kurdish, Education, and Linguistic Rights,* his most recent book, published by Tevn Press, Ozel has continued to advocate for and explore the Kurdish language. He is a founding member of the Kurdish Languağe Academy of Brussels and was on the board of the Istanbul Kurdish Institute for ten years, from 1994 to 2004. Ozel is also a distinguished English language instructor having written the popular *The Way to Cope with Proficiency Exams,* which assists Turkish students in preparing for English proficiency tests. He is the founder and director of Akademik Dil Ögretim Merkezi, his own English language academy in Ankara, Turkey where he currently resides.

Additional Contributors

Mustafa Dehqan

Mustafa Dehqan, who contributed the Goranî legend of "Rawchî," is an Iranian Kurd. In 1977, his parents were forced to move from Kurdistan to Tehran where, in 1978, Mustafa was born. They currently live in Karadj, a small city on the outskirts of Tehran. Mustafa holds a B.A. in historical studies and an M.A. in historical linguistics from the University of Tehran. To date, he has published a number of essays on Kurdish religion and language including his most recent "Allusions to Kurdish Community in Shiite Classical Literature." He is currently conducting a bibliographical research project on the Kurds in Medieval Arabic and Persian Literature.

Rudman Ham

The older photos used in this book were taken in Iraqi Kurdistan circa 1954–1956 and provided by Rudman Ham. After graduation from the University of New Hampshire in 1953, Rudman volunteered as a conscientious objector to work in the Middle East for two years in lieu of military service. He was assigned by International Voluntary Services to Shaqlawa, a Kurdish village in the mountains above Erbil, Iraq. From 1954 to 1956, this group of volunteers initiated demonstration projects in distributing clean water, improved dairy and egg production, and various public health programs. All photos were taken as colored slides with a Pony 828 Kodak Camera.

Zerî Înanç

The proverbs that introduce sections of this book were selected and translated by Zerî Înanç, a Kurdish writer and translator. Zerî has gathered four thousand Kurdish proverbs over more than ten years. She has several published works on Kurds and on minority rights. Her collection of proverbs will be published in the near future.

Yuksel Serindag

Yuksel was born in the Kurdish town of Cewlig in Turkish Kurdistan. It is an area surrounded by high mountains and rivers that give both the people and the town constant energy and life. Yuksel, like many people in Cewlig, speaks both Kurmancî and Dimilî. For this book, he helped with collections and translations of stories in both dialects. Nihat Elci from Cewlig was one that he interviewed extensively for this collection. He is currently employed at the Trinity College Library, Hartford, Connecticut, while he pursues his master's degree in library science at Queens College in Flushing, New York.

Leeya Thompson

Leeya Thompson contributed the story "Sultan Mahmud and Heyas." She has a number of books and scripts to her credit including the newly published *The Wisdom of Sound and Number*, an exploration of Chaldean numerology. In 1992–1993, Leeya had the opportunity to edit and retell the Soranî Kurdish folktales of Sheikh Tinue Berzinjî for her manuscript, *Winter Tales: A Collection of Kurdish Folktales*. It is hoped that her unique collection of Kurdish tales will be published soon.

Recent Titles in the
World Folklore Series

The Flying Dutchman and Other Folktales from the Netherlands
Theo Meder

Folktales from the Japanese Countryside
As told by Hiroko Fujita; Edited by Fran Stallings with Harold Wright and Miki Sakurai

Mayan Folktales; Cuentos Folklricos Mayas
Retold and Edited by Susank Conklin Thompson, Keith Thompson, and Lidia López de López

The Flower of Paradise and Other Armenian Tales
Translated and Retold by Bonnie C. Marshall; Edited and with a Foreword by Virginia Tashjian

The Magic Lotus Lantern and Other Tales from the Han Chinese
Haiwang Yuan

Brazilian Folktales
Livia de Almeida and Ana Portella; Edited by Margaret Read MacDonald

The Seven Swabians, and Other German Folktales
Anna Altmann

English Folktales
Edited by Dan Keding and Amy Douglas

The Snow Maiden and Other Russian Tales
Translated and Retold by Bonnie C. Marshall, Edited by Alla V. Kulagina

From the Winds of Manguito: Cuban Folktales in English and Spanish (Desde los vientos de Manguito: Cuentos folklóricos de Cuba, en inglés y español)
Retold by Elvia Perez, Edited by Margaret Read MacDonald

Tales from the Taiwanese
Retold by Gary Marvin Davison

Indonesian Folktales
Retold by Murti Bunanta, Edited by Margaret Read MacDonald

Additional titles in this series can be found at www.lu.com